Language Contact in Nepal

Bhim Lal Gautam

Language Contact in Nepal

A Study on Language Use and Attitudes

Bhim Lal Gautam
Central Department of Linguistics
Tribhuvan University
Kirtipur, Nepal

ISBN 978-3-030-68809-7   ISBN 978-3-030-68810-3   (eBook)
https://doi.org/10.1007/978-3-030-68810-3

This Palgrave Macmillan imprint is published by the registered company Springer Nature Switzerland AG.
The registered company address is: Gewerbestrasse 11, 6330 Cham, Switzerland

PREFACE

This book is the outcome of my own field and research experiences during the last fifteen years in Nepal. I have been involved in teaching and research activities at the Centre Department of Linguistics, Tribhuvan University since 2000. My research experiences for the documentation of minority and endangered languages of Nepal and various field visits during the sociolinguistic survey of Nepalese languages have been accumulated in this book. Various institutions including the Central Department of Linguistics, Tribhuvan University, University Grants Commission Nepal, Linguistic Survey of Nepal project (2008–2018), Language Commission Nepal and many others have supported me technically and financially in different periods during my research works that motivated me to compose this book. My own PhD research (2020) entitled *Language Contact in Kathmandu Valley* is also a crucial source of information.

There is not any reference material that deals with language contact study in the local context. There are numerous books in theoretical issues but not a book based on data and research. To the present, very little or no attempt has been made in the South Asian context to work in this area where bilingual/ multilingual activities are conditioned by social factors including power relations, normativity, political competition and network membership. My motivation to produce this book is for the new researchers to explore other areas of language contact studies in South Asia in general and Nepal in particular. In this context, this book is based on the mixed research method in order to find out the trends, causes and impacts of language contact and shift among the diverse speakers from the Kathmandu valley and outside Nepal.

This book will provide an opportunity for future researchers of South Asian languages to test the methodology of language contact study and to learn more about the languages of the subcontinent. This study of language contact phenomena in Nepal will enable researchers to document examples of language change among the respective speakers/ communities which may then serve as the basis of comparison with the linguistic varieties in the regions where these languages are traditionally spoken. It will also help us explore some common typological features of South Asian languages from a language contact perspective.

Kirtipur, Nepal   Bhim Lal Gautam

ACKNOWLEDGEMENTS

I would like to thank to all my friends, colleagues and senior linguists from Nepal and abroad who helped and inspired me to carry out this work. I shall never forget the help, cooperation and enthusiasm of the people, informants and activists from the different language communities during my field visit in Nepal.

I would like to express my thanks to University Grants Commission, Nepal and Language Commission Nepal for providing me with funds to carry out related researches discussed in this book.

I am heavily indebted to Ms. Liv Godal from Norway who constantly helped and supported me financially during my research. My special thanks go to Anetta Kopecka and Colette Grinevald (DDL, University of Lyon 2, France) for providing me with an ASLAN Fellowship (2014) in order to develop the background and tools for this research. I feel greatly honored by the theoretical and conceptual feedback from Hans Hock (Illinois, USA), Susan Gal (USA), Tanmoy Bhattacharya (DU, India), Anju Saksena (Uppsala, Sweden), Dan Raj Regmi (TU, Nepal) and John Peterson (Kiel, Germany) during my period of research on language contact. Last but not least, my special thanks goes to three reviewers, and to Cathy Scott and Alice Green from Palgrave Macmillan for helping with so many things during the process of manuscript revision of the book.

Bhim Lal Gautam, PhD

CONTENTS

ABBREVIATIONS

AA	Austro Asiatic
BBC	British Broadcasting Corporation
CBS	Central Bureau of Statistics
CDL	Central Department of Linguistics
CNN	Cable News Network
CS	Communal Solidarity
DDL	Laboratoire Dynamique du Langage
FGD	Focus Group Discussion
IA	Indo-Aryan language
LWC	Language of Wider Communication
MT	Mother Tongue
NEPC	New Education Planning Commission
RLS	Reversing Language Shift
SL	Source language
TB	Tibeto-Burman language
TL	Target language
TU	Tribhuvan University
UK	United Kingdom
UNESCO	United Nations Educational, Scientific and Cultural Organization
USA	United States of America

LIST OF FIGURES

LIST OF TABLES

CHAPTER 1

Introduction

This book is based up on the findings of various research works conducted by the author over the period 2005–2019 in Nepal. Various research activities at the Central department of linguistics, Tribhuvan University, University Grants Commission Nepal, Linguistic Survey of Nepal Project (2008–2018) where I took part in fieldwork and research motivated me to produce this book. My own PhD thesis, *Language Contact in Kathmandu Valley*, is a key source of this book.

The book consists of eight chapters: Chap. 1 is an introduction to the book and the methodology used to collect data; Chap. 2 describes the sociolinguistic and multilingual situation of Nepal; Chap. 3 outlines the language contact politics of Nepal, and provides information about the studies in this area; Chaps. 4, 5 and 6 describe the language contact situation of Kathmandu Valley, focusing on the language use and attitude of Sherpa, Newar and Maithili speakers; Chap. 7 introduces the general patterns of language shift in Nepal; Chap. 8 deals with language contact and its implications for language policies.

The research on which the book is based followed a mixed method, paying equal attention to quantitative and qualitative approaches in order to discover the trends, causes and impacts of language contact and shift among speakers from the valley and outside Nepal. Some numerical data were collected to show changes in the number of speakers of different languages through a quantitative lens, while the perceptions and attitudes of the speakers were scrutinized by means of qualitative tools. The aim of

© The Author(s), under exclusive license to Springer Nature
Switzerland AG 2021
B. L. Gautam, *Language Contact in Nepal*,
https://doi.org/10.1007/978-3-030-68810-3_1

the qualitative research was to find out answer to the question "How and why do people think and behave" in a particular way (Ambert et al. 1995: 88).The study was mainly based on the data collected through the use of a survey questionnaire,[1] focus group discussion (FGD) and informal interview. Homogeneous sampling technique was employed in the research where the units (people, cases etc.) share the same characteristics or traits. Informal observation technique was used to elicit qualitative data. Qualitative techniques were used to understand people's own views of and approaches to the use of mother tongues, including Nepali, Newar, Sherpa, Maithili, Tharu, Jumli and Dotyali. In order to maintain ethics in the field confidentiality was maintained in everything that the author came to know about informants. Interviews were taken and FGDs conducted only at times convenient to the respondents, and the researcher ended questioning talking when participants showed clear signs of boredom. The interviews were resumed in a convenient time and place. The research used a mixed methodology, including ethnographic research involving both fieldwork in various communities and the gathering of different types of data through attitude studies, interviews and recordings.

The sites selected and populations sampled do not represent the overall situation of Nepal and Kathmandu Valley but rather seek to address the indicative features of language contact in the selected sites (Flick 2009). In the study, respondents' perceptions of the use of languages for various purposes provided a framework for analyzing language contact and shift in the selected sites. Although survey forms were used for collecting quantitative data and analyzed in Excel, they have also been interpreted and analyzed by different qualitative methods.

The questionnaires were translated into Nepali and administered to the concerned informants. There were 255 questionnaires completed altogether. Of them, 135 were for language contact in Kathmandu Valley and 120 for language shift in Nepal. They contained metadata information and questions on language use and attitude. Chapters 3, 4 and 5 are based on data drawn from 135 questionnaires, different FGDs, observations and informal interviews collected from the Kathmandu Valley. Chapter 6 on language shift is based on data drawn from 120 questionnaires completed in different provincial areas—the Far Western, Karnali, Bagmati and Terai regions of Nepal. Those items included the Dotyali, Jumli, Tharu and Nepali languages. The names and gender of the informants have been anonymized for privacy, and pseudonyms are used. Moreover, the book also draws on some existing literature related to language contact and shift.

This book provides a relatively comprehensive synthesis of the language contact politics of Nepal, with sufficient research data on language use and attitude in descriptive way. It can be a reference guide for early-career researchers and for people who are interested in the sociolinguistics of multilingualism in Nepal. The data and research in Kathmandu Valley among Sherpa, Newar and Maithili speakers represent the urban language dynamic in a multilingual capital city which can be compared with the similar situations throughout the world. Similarly, research on Dotyali, Jumli and Tharu language communities outside the capital city indicate the general trend of language contact and shift in a multilingual country. The languages were selected to find out the intra-lingual (Dotyali and Jumli) and inter-lingual (Sherpa, Newar, Tharu, Maithili) contact phenomena in the Nepalese context.

NOTE

1. The questionnaire was developed in 2014 by the author in DDL, University of Lyon 2, France and the pilot testing was done in 2015 in Kathmandu.

BIBLIOGRAPHY

Ambert, A. M., Adler, P. A., Adler., & Detzner, D. F. (1995). Understanding and evaluating qualitative research. *Journal of marriage and the family, 57*(4), 879–893.

Flick. (2009). *An introduction to qualitative research* (4th ed.). Thousand Oaks, CA: Sage Publications Ltd.

CHAPTER 2

Sociolinguistics of Multilingualism in Nepal

2.1   Introduction

This chapter sheds lights on the current sociolinguistic situation in Nepal, focusing on the notions of multilingualism and language contact. It deals with the major dimensions of sociolinguistics and multilingualism in the country and attempts to present an overview of Nepal's linguistic diversity based on the latest information about the status and vitality of Nepalese languages. Furthermore, it analyzes the existing language provisions in the constitution and language policy of Nepal. It also offers a brief history of the Nepali language and its contact with many other languages including English over time. The subsequent discussion incorporates various ideological and sociocultural aspects of language contact and shift in a multilingual setting.

2.2   Linguistic Diversity and Language Vitality in Nepal

Nepal is diverse in culture, language, ethnicity and ecology. According to the 2011 census, Nepal has more than 123 languages, which can be classified into four major language families: the Tibeto-Burman branch of Sino-Tibetan, the Indo-Aryan branch of Indo-European, Austro-Asiatic and Dravidian and a language isolate called Kusunda. Multilingualism is a

B. L. Gautam, *Language Contact in Nepal*, https://doi.org/10.1007/978-3-030-68810-3_2

unique natural and historical feature of Nepalese identity. Linguistic, cultural and ethnic diversities have been the essence of Nepalese society for centuries.

Linguistic diversity is closely related to ecological and cultural diversity. The concept of ecosystem is guided by the principle that living entities exist through a linkage of inter-relationships. The domains of biological, linguistic and cultural diversities hold a mutually reinforcing connection. Nepal is a home to over 5400 species of higher plants and 850 species of birds measuring about 2.2% and 9.4% of the world's level of biodiversity per unit area, matched by a similar rate of linguistic and cultural variation (Turin 2007). Human success in dwelling the Earth has been due to the human ability to develop diverse cultures and languages which suit all kinds of environments. Now it may be argued that if diversity is an essential to successful humanity then the preservation of linguistic diversity is crucial to humanity. Crystal (2000) argues that if the development of multiple cultures is so important then the role of languages becomes critical, for cultures are chiefly transmitted through spoken and written languages (p. 34). Further, various languages serve as symbols of ethnic identity, and every speech community wishes to preserve and promote its language.

The great biological diversity of present-day Nepal is matched by its cultural and linguistic diversity. Comprising an area of 147,516 square kilometers,[1] with a length of 885 kilometers from east to west and a breadth of 193 kilometers from north to south, the topography of Nepal is rich and varied. Inhabiting these different climatic and ecological zones are 125 officially recognized caste and ethnic groups who speak 125-plus languages officially recognized by the state and a few further unidentified languages (Yadava 2014). Table 2.1 presents a brief synopsis of the ethnic diversity of Nepal.

Table 2.1 indicates that the languages spoken in Nepal have been categorized in relation to different ethnicities and religions. Ten different ethnic groups such as Brahmin, Chhetri, Thakuri, Kami and Sanyasi speak Nepali as a common mother tongue. Fifty-three other ethnic groups speak Newar, Tamang, Limbu, Sherpa, Thakali, Kumal, Majhi, Dhimal, Byansi, Satar and other languages. Similarly, five ethnic groups speak more than one language. These languages include Magar (Kham, Kaike, Poike, Dhut), Chepang (Bankariya, Chepang), Gurung (Ghale, Gurung) and Rai (Bantawa, Chamling, Kulung, Yamphu, Thulung).Many ethnic groups living in the Terai region of Nepal speak three major languages viz. Maithili, Bhojpuri and Awadhi. They include the Yadava, Musahar, Teli,

Table 2.1 Ethnic diversity of Nepal

SN	Language condition/Structure	Number of ethnicities	Mother tongue
1	Many ethnicities one language	10	Nepali
2	One ethnicity one language	53	Newar, Tamang, Limbu, Sherpa, Kumal, etc.
3	One ethnicity many languages	5	Magar, Chepang, and Gurung
4	One ethnicity but different languages	40	Maithili, Bhojpuri, Awadhi, Bajjika, Maghai, etc.
5	Unidentified	17	

Source: Extracted from Yadava (2014) and CBS (2011)

Table 2.2 Population of major language families in Nepal

SN	Language Family	Number of Languages	Number of speakers	Percentage of speakers
1	Indo European	49	21,755,300	82.11%
2	Tibeto-Burman	70	4,586,538	17.31%
3	Austro Asiatic	2	50,096	0.19%
4	Dravidian	1	33,651	0.13%
5	Language Isolate	1	28	0.00%
6	Others		21,173	0.07%
7	Unidentified		47,718	0.18%
Grand Total		123	26,494,504	100%

Source: *Population of Nepal by Mother Tongue* (CBS 2011)

Chamar, Kurmi, Lohar, Rajput, Kayastha and Thakur ethnic groups. However, many other languages and ethnicities have not yet been identified.

2.2.1   The Status of Nepal's Languages

Languages spoken in Nepal have been classified in different language families and groups which are presented in Table 2.2. The table also shows the population of the speakers of major language families in Nepal.

Table 2.2 shows the number of speakers of the major languages, the number of which increased from 92 to 123 languages in the 2011 census.

This uncertainty about the number of Nepal's languages and their reduced enumeration in the previous five censuses may be attributed to a lack of required information and awareness about mother tongues and the absence of a suitable language policy in Nepal.

2.2.2   Writing Systems

Most of the indigenous languages spoken in Nepal are still confined to their oral traditions. Each of them has a rich oral heritage of traditional folk stories and songs transmitted from parent to child over a long period of time, such as the *Mundhum*[2] in Kiranti languages. However, these oral tales are disappearing with the growth of literacy and with increased language contact and shift. It is, therefore, time to document these spoken forms before they are lost to future generations.

Only a few of Nepal's indigenous languages have literary traditions. These include, among others, Sherpa, Newar, Limbu, Lepcha, Maithili and Tamang. Table 2.3 presents a summary of the scripts used in Nepal.

Table 2.3   Major Scripts in Nepal

SN	Script	Languages
1	Devanagari	Nepali, Maithili, Bhojpuri, Awadhi, Newar, Rajbansi, Magar, Tamang and Kirati
2	Mithilachhyar/ Tirahuta	Maithili
3	Kaithi	Maithili
4	Sambota	Tibetan, Sherpa, Tamang, Lohwa, Seke
5	Tamahik	Tamang
6	Ranjana	Newar
7	Sirijanga	Limbu
8	Rong	Lepcha
9	Akkha	Magar
10	Gurumukhi	Panjabi
11	Arabian	Urdu
12	Latin/Roman	Santhali/Gurung
13	Ol Chemel/ Ol Chiki/Ol	Santhali
14	Khema	Gurung
15	Bangla	Bangali

Source: Yadava and Turin (2005)

These languages have long traditions of written literature and have employed various writing systems or scripts. Tibetan and Sherpa are two of the Tibeto-Burman languages with the earliest written records. The Tibetan script was developed from the Gupta or Brahmi script, which was employed for writing Sanskrit in the mid-seventh century.

Newar (or *Nepal Bhasha*[3]) is another Tibeto-Burman language with an ancient written literary tradition. Newar script was introduced around the ninth century and was used in most of the earlier documents written in Kathmandu Valley; from it emerged other Newari scripts in the forms of Ranjana and Bhujimol. Ranjana was in fashion from the eleventh to the eighteenth centuries, while Bhujimol remained in use from the eleventh to the seventeenth centuries. A number of other scripts used for writing the Newar language emerged from the Bhujimol script. These scripts are referred to as Golmol, Litumol, Kwemol, Kunmol, Hinmol and Pachumol, and are supposed to have been introduced by Newar scholars for writing ornamental texts on specific festivals and ritual occasions. These elaborated scripts were introduced in the thirteenth century and continued to be used until the seventeenth century (Malla 2015). Today, the Newar language is also written in the Devanagri script for the sake of convenience in reading, writing and printing. Limbu, another Tibeto-Burman language, uses its own Kiranti *Sirijanga* script. Lepcha is written in Rong script. Both of these scripts were developed to propagate Buddhism during the regime of the third Chögyal or "Maharaja" of Sikkim.

More recently, some of Nepal's indigenous languages have begun to develop literary traditions. Initiatives have been taken by various language communities to develop writing systems appropriate to the sound system of their languages and which are practical and acceptable to them. These speech communities include Tharu, Tamang, Magar, Gurung, Rajbanshi and a subset of the Rai group of languages such as Bantawa, Thulung, Chamling, Khaling, Kulung and others. Tharu, Tamang and Gurung languages use the Devanagri script, but some Gurung speakers advocate the use of the Roman script for their language. Magar has developed its own script, called Akkha. Recently, these languages have begun to develop written literature in the form of newspapers, magazines, textbooks for adult literacy and primary education, as well as folk literature. As in India, Santhali spoken in Nepal can be written in Roman script.

2.2.3   Language Vitality in Nepal

Language vitality is an indicator of a language's sustainability, and of the magnitude to which interference is required for its maintenance. Vitality is not a property of a language itself, nor of a population that speaks a language, but rather it is a description of the relationship between a language, its speakers and its broader linguistic, social and political context. It therefore reflects how the overall language ecology influences individual languages and its speakers. We can see an appealing situation of language vitality in the context of Nepal. There are two major contributing factors to language shift and endangerment in Nepal. The first is the complex ethno-linguistic situation generated by the entangled relationship of the diverse languages of the different ethnicities and religions. The second is the unequal distribution of the number of speakers among the major language families. Indo-European, with 80.12% of speakers, is the largest language family in terms of speakers. Due to increasing ethnic consciousness among communities, especially after the restoration of democracy in 1990, the number of ethnic languages is gradually increasing in Nepal. The 2011 census of Nepal recorded more than 83 ethnic languages out of a total of 123 or more languages. The number was 70-plus in the 2001 census (CBS 2002). However, the percentage of ethnic language speakers has considerably decreased (Sino-Tibetan languages were spoken by 18.86% of the total population in 2001 but only 17.31% in 2011), reflecting speakers shifting to Nepali (Regmi 2015).

The 2011 census reveals an increasing number of languages in Nepal. At the same time, the number of endangered languages has also increased, which indicates that measures taken to preserve those languages are ineffective. Hence, realistic and effective measures need to be immediately taken by the concerned authorities and the speech communities. Figure 2.1 presents an assessment of the vitality of the languages of Nepal based on the Expanded Graded Intergenerational Disruption Scale model proposed by Lewis and Simons (2010).

Figure 2.1 shows that fewer than 44% (53) of languages are vigorous/safe. More than 41% (51) of languages are threatened, i.e., only child-bearing generations are transmitting these languages to their children. Likewise, 8.9% (11) of languages are shifting and 4.87% (6) are moribund. Finally, 0.8% (1) is nearly extinct and 0.8% (1) is dormant. Generally, more than 56% of Nepal's languages are facing different levels of endangerment.

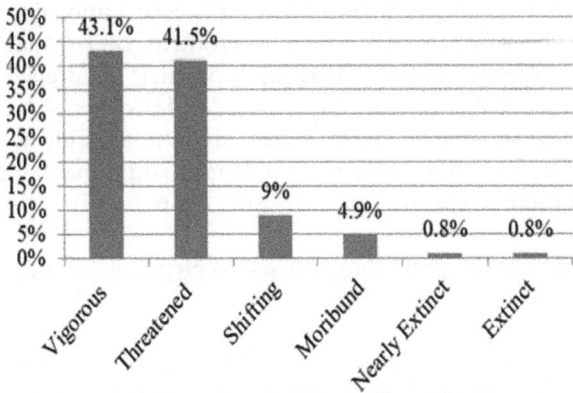

Fig. 2.1 Vitality of languages in Nepal. (Source: Regmi 2017)

2.3 EXISTING LANGUAGE PROVISION AND POLICY IN NEPAL

Despite being multicultural and multilingual, Nepal preserved "ethnic," rather than "civic," nationalism in its task of nation-building, and this is reflected in various subsidiary governments in the country. Following the Gorkha conquest, Gorkhali or Khas, the language of ruling elites, also spoken by hill people as a lingua franca or mother tongue, assumed the new terminology "Nepali" with an intent of transforming it into the official national language. The Rana regime further promoted this "one nation, one language" policy. This was a deliberate plan to eliminate all but one language, viz. Nepali. This is evident from the fact that Newar- and Hindi-language movements were suppressed. Notably, the following recommendations formed Nepal's first language policy in education (NEPC 1956):

1. The medium of instruction should be the national language in primary, middle, and higher educational institutions, because any language that cannot be made lingua franca and does not serve legal proceedings in court should be developed and should not be preserved. The use of national language can bring about equality among all classes of people, can be an anchor-sheet for Nepalese nationality, and can be the main instrument for promoting literature.

2. No other languages should be taught, even optionally, in primary
   school because few children will need them, they would hinder the
   use of Nepali, parents would insist on their children taking them
   whether capable or not, time is needed for other more important
   and fundamental learning—there are not enough well-qualified
   teachers, and those who wish and need additional languages, can
   begin them in the 6th grade. (NEPC 1956, p. 95)

The motive behind prescribing the use of Nepali alone is clear from the
following extract:

> If the younger generation is taught to use Nepali as the basic language then
> other languages will gradually disappear, the greater the national strength
> and unity will be extended. So that local dialects and tongues other than
> Nepali should be vanished [banished] from the playground as early as pos-
> sible in the life of the child. (NEPC 1956; as cited in Gurung 2002 and
> Maddox 2003)

The use of Nepali in education was further reinforced by the action of
the K.I. Singh government in 1957 of prescribing Nepali as the medium
of instruction. This instance shows the nationalist language policy of
the past.

The case of Nepali was further reinforced during the Panchayat regime.
In 1961, the National System of Education was introduced to further
promote the use solely of Nepali in administration, education and media,
in compliance with the Panchayat slogan "one language, one dress, one
country" (*eutaa bhasha, eutaa bhesh, eutaa desh*). In addition, the Nepali
Company Act was passed in 1964 directing all companies to keep their
records in English or Nepali. The Panchayat constitution featured a language assimilation policy which promoted the Nepali language in many
different ways.

However, Nepal's political revolution in 1990 brought significant
changes in Nepalese society in terms of freedom and human rights. With
the restoration of democracy there has been growing awareness among
non-Nepali speaking people about their culture and languages since they
consider them as the symbols through which they strive to assert their
identity and recognition. The 1991 Constitution of Nepal, framed after
the restoration of democracy, recognized languages other than Nepali and
made the following provisions about non-Nepali languages:

1. The Nepali language in the Devanagari script is the language of the nation of Nepal. The Nepali language shall be the official language. (Constitution of Nepal, Part 1, Article 6.1)
2. All the languages spoken as a mother tongue in the various parts of Nepal are the national languages of Nepal. (Constitution of Nepal, Part 1, Article 6.2)

In addition, the 1991 Constitution made a provision for the use of mother tongues in primary education (Constitution of Nepal, Part 1, Article 18.2). It also guaranteed a fundamental right to people to preserve their culture, scripts and languages (Constitution of Nepal, Part 1, Article 26.2).

Similarly, the Maoist revolution that started in 1996 brought new changes and dynamics to all the ethnic minorities of Nepal. This political campaign motivated them to preserve and promote their languages and cultures, and this is acknowledged in the Interim Constitution of Nepal (2007). The Interim Constitution, an outcome of the people's revolution (*Andolan II*), makes the following provisions for languages:

1. All the languages spoken as a mother tongue in Nepal are the national languages of Nepal.
2. The Nepali Language in Devnagari script shall be the official language.
3. Notwithstanding anything contained in clause (2), it shall not be deemed to be a hindrance to use a mother language in local bodies and offices. The state shall translate the languages when they are used for official purpose. (Interim Constitution of Nepal (2007), Part 1, Article 5)

Regarding education and cultural rights, the Interim Constitution enshrines the following provisions:

1. Each community shall have the right to receive basic education in their mother tongue as provided for in the law.
2. Each community residing in Nepal shall have the right to preserve and promote its language, script, culture, cultural civility and heritage. (Interim Constitution of Nepal (2007), Part 3, Article 17)

The Interim Constitution of Nepal was more progressive and liberal than the constitution of 1991. For the first time, all the languages spoken in Nepal were recognized as national languages. Apart from further confirming the right of each community residing in Nepal to preserve and promote its language, script, culture, cultural civility and heritage, the Interim Constitution clearly recognized the right of each community to basic education in their mother tongue. However, the role of the government in facilitating speech communities to materialize these rights has so far been ineffective.

The latest Constitution of Nepal (2015) includes the following provisions:

1. Languages of the nation: All languages spoken as mother tongues in Nepal are the languages of the nation. (Part 1, Article 6)
2. Official language: (1) The Nepali language in the Devanagari script shall be the official language of Nepal.
3. A State may, by a State law, determine one or more than one languages of the nation spoken by a majority of people within the State to be its official language(s), in addition to the Nepali language.
4. Other matters relating to language shall be as decided by the Government of Nepal, on recommendation of the Language Commission. (Part 1, Article7)

The 2015 Constitution has conferred the right to basic education in mother tongue (Article 31 (1)), right to use mother language (Article 32 (1)) and preservation and promotion of language (Article 32(3)). It states that every community residing in Nepal shall have the right to preserve and promote its language, script, culture, cultural civility and heritage. However, unless the constitution articulates the responsibility of the government to preserve and promote the endangered languages, the efforts of the communities will be useless. Observing and analyzing the legal provisions from the beginning to the present time, Nepal has made significant progress and gradual changes along with historical events. The key measure of a language's viability is not the number of people who speak it, but the extent to which children are still learning the language as their native tongue.

2.4   The Role of the Nepali Language

The Nepali language is the dominant and most widely spoken language in Nepal. It is the first language of 44.6% of the country's population (CBS 2011). The rest of the population speaks Nepali as a second language in inter-group communication in addition to their own mother tongue, which they use in intra-ethnic group communication. Thus, the aforementioned percentage of speakers speaking the Nepali language as a first language is a combination of the speakers from both the Brahmin and Chhetri caste groups and from other ethnic groups.

According to the census of 2011 the Chhetri comprised 16.6% and the Brahmin 12.2% of the total Nepalese population of 26.5 million. That is, these groups, both of which speak Nepali as a first language, made up nearly 29% of the total population. The remaining 16% of the population who speak Nepali as a first language came from other ethnic groups. However, the proportion of Nepali speakers has fallen from 58.4% of a total population of 15 million in 1991. This is evidence that ethnic groups have started to exhibit affiliation to their own languages, though many cannot speak them fluently. They wish to identify themselves with their languages and cultures. As in other countries, ethnic languages have an identity-building function in Nepal.

Although studies on the comprehension and the use of Nepali by non-Nepali speakers are far and few between, sheer expediency seems to have driven more and more non –Nepali speakers to use and understand it in their day-to-day transactions, inter-ethnic communications and above all in their communication with the channels of the local and national administration.

In all these avenues of communication, some forms of Nepali have been used for the last two centuries. The rise of Nepali, first as a lingua franca in the wake of the Gorkhali military campaign (1742–1814), then its continuous use as the language of authority and administration, made Nepali an unchallenged national language of Nepal by the people, constitution and authority.

In this relatively newly formed state, the Nepali language was promoted as necessary for unifying all of the Nepalese people irrespective of their different languages and cultures. The Shah rulers, rejecting the mosaic of ethnic languages and cultures, imposed linguistic dominance by placing ethnic groups under Nepali-speaking elites through internal colonization (Riaz and Basu 2007: 70). Nepal was declared an exclusive Hindu kingdom, denying the existence of all the ethnic languages. The state did not take a positive approach to any of Nepal's other existing languages and cultures.

Because the Nepali language has for so long been used more widely than any other ethnic languages it was recognized as the language of the nation and lingua franca first, then as an official and national language (Bandhu 1989: 121).

2.5   FACTORS SUPPORTING NEPALI AS THE NATIONAL LANGUAGE

The designation of Nepali as the national language can be traced back to a number of political, religious, cultural and economic factors.

2.5.1   Political Factors

The suppression of the country's ethnic languages began with the unification of Nepal also known as the expansion campaign of the Gorkha Kingdom by the founder of the Shah Dynasty, King Prithvi Narayan Shah. He imposed the Nepali language and Hindu religion on small ethnic states with their own distinctive cultures, languages and religions, and which had been annexed by invasion. All of the ethnic subjects were obliged to obey four fundamental principles based on caste, ethnicity and profession of people known as *charjata*.[4] Nepalese subjects were prohibited from questioning the authority of the Hindu king of Gorkha, the Hindu culture, the Hindu hierarchical caste systems and Nepali as the language of administration and education (Tumbahang 2009: 7).

Ethnic groups continued facing linguistic suppression during the Rana oligarchy and the Panchayat System, which introduced the policy of "One nation, one culture, one language" from 1962 to 1989. During these decades the government became indifferent to ethnic languages (Yadava and Turin 2005; Paudel 2009).King Rana Bahadur Shah ordered the Limbus in government offices to correspond in Nepali language. Ethnic languages in Nepal did not have the same political capital as Nepali, reflecting the observation of Carol Myers-Scotton (2002) "those languages with the greatest capital are the languages of government business and the medium of higher education" (p. 35). The elites, such as government and educated language policy makers, did not allocate official and other public functions to the other ethnic languages. They excluded them from the national language policy. Ram Mani Acharya Dixit, a member of the Gorkha (Nepali) Language Publication Committee, destroyed the genealogies, and copper and stone written inscriptions of ethnic people, along with burning 30,000 hand written documents related to language, script, culture and religion in 1913 (Gurung 1985; Neupane 2010).These actions are evidence of the influence of political factors.

2.5.2   Religious Factors

The Hindu rulers did not want to preserve and promote Nepal's ethnic languages (Tumbahang 2009: 14). The Ranas perpetuated a policy of Hinduization which systematized the incorporation of Nepal's many disparate ethno-linguistic groups into a national hierarchy of castes and ethnic groups headed by the Khas (later called Chhetri and Bahuns or Brahmins) of the Gorkhali elites (Hutt 2004: 2). For instance, three municipalities declared languages other than Nepali as official languages: Kathmandu declared Nepal Bhasa or the Newar language, as an official language, and Dhanusha and Rajbiraj district declared Maithili as the official language. However, the Supreme Court of Nepal issued a verdict denouncing the decision of the three districts on June 1, 1999. Even though the declarations made by the municipalities/ districts were in accordance with the legal provisions of the Self-Governance Act of 1999, they lost the legal battle against the government. Hinduization or Sanskritization played a huge role in suppressing Nepal's ethnic languages and cultures.

2.5.3   Economic Factors

Population mobility also has to be taken into consideration when discussing the linguistic situation of Nepal. People migrated for economic reasons: thus, rural Nepalese relocated to such cities as Kathmandu and assumed de-ethnicized urban identities. They felt proud of being permanent residents of a big city like Kathmandu. In Nepal, speaking Nepali became associated with high-income groups, not ethnic identity (Eagle 2000: 21).

Most ethnic groups traditionally resided in the mountainous area. This area scarcely contains enough cultivated land to produce sufficient subsistence crops to feed its inhabitants throughout the year. Moreover, crops are susceptible to destruction by natural calamities, such as landslides and floods. Consequently, many people from the mountainous areas of Nepal feel compelled to migrate to cities on the plains in the southern part of Nepal for better opportunities. This has led to a wave of economic migration to the cities, where original ethno-linguistic habits have changed, including a language shift to Nepali.

2.5.4   Sociocultural Factors

One of the most important drivers of the development and flourishing of the Nepali language in Nepalese society is the sociocultural factor. Nepalese society is basically Hindu-dominated, so most of the Hindu festivals such as Dashain, Tihar, Maghe Sanskranti and Chaite Dashain are common to all people, including those having different religions and ethnicities. Nepali language has become the common Nepali tongue outside in the Diasporas. Every Nepali outside Nepal—in the United Kingdom, Hong Kong, Burma, India, the United States and many other countries—celebrates various Nepalese festivals by sharing and caring for other Nepalis. In these occasions, most of the communications and transactions are made in Nepali language.

2.6   THE NEPALI LANGUAGE IN CONTACT WITH ENGLISH

The Nepali language has been in contact with English as well as the other languages spoken in the country since the time of unification movement in Nepal. When Prithvi Narayan Shah conquered Kathmandu Valley Nepali became the language of power, law and administration. Nepali–English language contact is associated with the territorial expansion of Nepal, which was pursued militarily but ended after the encounter with British India in 1816. After signing a treaty with British India, Gorkhali expansionist military power was limited to the symbol of the royal army: the "*khukuri cross*" (Hachhethu 2003: 221). Hence, the treaty accounts for English–Nepali language contact. Native English speakers also came and stayed in Nepal on diplomatic missions which further facilitated Nepali–English contact.

The status of the English language in Nepal is different from that of Nepali. The Nepali language was imposed by the government top to down (i.e., all levels of agencies) (Simpson 2007: 15). In contrast, English-speaking has developed gradually through the language contact situation and its use by growing numbers of Nepali citizens.

Nepali-speaking people first came into contact with English-speakers on the arrival of the British missionaries, Father Craybrawl in 1628, and Father Grover and Father Dorbil in 1661. Their primary mission was to preach the Christian gospel and convert the Nepali people to Christianity (Sharma 2000: 33). The missionaries, who were allowed to stay in Kathmandu Valley by the Malla rulers, left the country after the Malla kings surrendered to the Shah King, Prithvi Narayan Shah in the early eighteenth century. The missionaries were obliged to leave by the antagonistic policy toward foreign nationals adopted by the then Shah ruler, as stated in the *Divya Upadesh* (the Divine counsel). Though the stay of the missionaries in Kathmandu Valley was short this was the first contact of Nepalis with the English language.

Due to the lack of a concrete plan by the Nepalese government regarding the development of the ethnic languages, the English language, along with Nepali, has come to be predominant in school curricula, in both the rural and urban parts of Nepal. The learning of English improves Nepalis' opportunities of obtaining jobs in national and international governmental organizations and in the media. Hence the attraction felt by a large section of the Nepalese people to the English language rather than other local languages.

Learning English is deeply rooted among Nepalese across the country, despite the fact that the government has been reluctant to use English as a medium of instruction formally and officially. In the 1970s, the Nepalese government restructured the education system, with a view to limiting the scope of English education to specific purposes only. However, the use of the English language was revived country-wide in the education, business and tourism sectors after the establishment of multi-party democracy in 1990, and, notably, Tribhuvan University changed its policy and encouraged the use of English at various levels of its constituent campuses (Bhattarai 2006).

2.7   Code Switching/Mixing Among Various Languages

In the Nepalese context, various parameters for code switching/ mixing have been applied because of diverse sociocultural practices. Ethnic identity as well as the role of national and international languages with the impact of globalization created many language-contact situations in Nepal.

The languages which a multilingual person "mixes" contribute to placing him/her in the hierarchy of the social network in which he/she functions in order to socialize; code-mixing also marks their attitude and relationship toward the participants in a speech act and, consequently, the attitudes of the other participants toward him/her.

Different kinds of code-mixing and switching situations are available among the youth and educated community living in the city areas. Various studies of code switching/ mixing (Gautam and Sapkota 2005; Shah 2012; Yadav 2013, 2015) suggest that there is much switching between Nepali, English, Hindi and many local languages like Newar, Maithili, Bhojpuri, Tharu and so on. The reflection of code switching can be observed in media (radio and television) presentations on various musical and cultural activities. Code switching in Nepal is shifting towards Nepali and English among the minority and other language communities as a mark of modernization, high socioeconomic position, and identity with a certain type of elite group; and in stylistic terms it marks what may be termed "deliberate" style. A marker of "modernization" or civilization is the impact of western music and culture in Nepal. One can examine the features of the code-mixing of some Nepalese languages spoken in the Terai region such as Maithili, Tharu, Bhojpuri, Awadhi with Hindi and Nepali because of the influence of Indian music and television programs. This identifies a person in terms of their religion and/or occupation. The multilingual context of Nepal has created lots of opportunities for choosing codes. Because of inter- and intra-ethnic communication, the impact of education and literacy, media and marketing we find the people are using mixed forms of languages in many aspects of Nepalese society. Another very important reason for code switching/ mixing is the neoliberal influence of language because of globalization and urbanization. Nepalese people may speak different languages to communicate with a range of generations: mother tongue with their grandparents, Nepali and mother tongues with parents, Nepali and English with brothers and sisters and children.

2.8   LANGUAGE CHOICE AND FAMILY BILINGUALISM

The most important factor in maintaining family bilingualism appears to be the attitudes of the parents towards bilingualism and their desire to retain contact with their cultural background. Family bilingualism seldom arises totally spontaneously; in most cases it is the result of a conscious decision on the part of the parents to raise their children bilingually and a conscious effort to maintain bilingualism in the family. In a mixed-language marriage situation, the father often remarks that he feels it important that his children also learnt their parents' language so that they may identify with their cultural background. Ethnic and cultural background is often identified with solid moral values and discipline and Nepali and English background with a broader, more liberal perspective on life.

Language choice often depends on the values that parents wish to instill in their children. Parents who opt for bilingual homes usually feel that they are offering their children the best of both worlds. Many of the parents interviewed felt that to be bilingual was to be a more complete person with a better understanding of the values and aspirations of both language groups.

Instrumental motivation was another important factor for maintaining bilingualism. Most parents realized the need for children to be fluent in two languages. This was particularly common in homes where Nepali was the more dominant language. The parents wanted the children to learn English and go to English-medium schools because of the international, commercial and academic value of English.

Environmental factors also seem to play a role in the maintenance of bilingualism. One family retained their bilingualism because, despite using English in the home, they were involved in work environments where they had daily contact with Nepali and English speakers and were frequently in contact with their Nepali-speaking relatives. Another family lived in a bilingual environment in the cities and sent their children to a dual-medium school which supported their family bilingualism in their home. When they moved to their home and sent their children to an English-medium school, the level of bilingualism in the home started to decline. Sometimes environmental factors like fashion, mobility or migration can have an adverse effect on the home languages. One mixed-marriage family used Newar at their home when they were living in the predominantly English environment of Kathmandu, but when they moved to their home, there was a shift towards English to counterbalance the Newar influence outside the home (Gautam 2020).

NOTES

1. The Government of Nepal on May 18, 2020 (5th Jestha 2077) endorsed the new map including Lipulekh and Kalapani area with a new total area of 147,516 square kilometers.
2. Religious text of the Kiranti people.
3. The official name recognized by the Nepal government.
4. This indicates four castes: Brahmin, Chhetri, Basishya and Chhudra.

BIBLIOGRAPHY

Bandhu, C. M. (1989). The role of national language in establishing the national unity. *Kailash, 15*, 121–134.

Bhattarai, G. B. (2006). English teaching situation in Nepal: Elaboration of The theme for panel discussion in the 40th TESOL conference. *Journal of NELTA, 11*, 17–23.

Central Bureau of Statistics. (2002). *National population and housing census-2001.* Kathmandu: Central Bureau of Statistics, National Planning Commission (NPC).

Central Bureau of Statistics. (2011). *Population of Nepal.* Kathmandu: National Planning Commission.

Crystal, D. (2000). *Language death.* Cambridge: Cambridge University Press.

Eagle, S. (2000). The language situation in Nepal. In R. B. Baldauf & R. B. Kaplan (Eds.), *Language Planning in Nepal, Taiwan and Sweden* (pp. 170–225). Sydney: Multilingual Matters Ltd.

Gautam, B. L. (2020). *Language contact in Kathmandu.* An unpublished PhD dissertation, Tribhuvan University, Kathmandu.

Gautam, B. L., & Sapkota, S. (2005). A linguistic analysis of online communication. In *Contemporary Issues in Nepalese linguistics Vol. 21*, a journal of the Linguistic Society of Nepal (LSN).

Gurung, G. (1985). *Nepalko rajnitima adekhai sachai (Hidden truth in Nepalese politics).* Kathmandu: Gopal Gurung.

Gurung, H. (2002). *Janagananaa-2001 anusaar jaatiya tathyaank: prarambhik lekhaajokhaa* (Primary statistics of ethnicity according to census 2001). Kathmandu: Dhramodaya Sabha.

Hachhethu, K. (2003). Democracy and nationalism: Interface between state and Ethnicity in Nepal. *Contribution to Nepalese Studies, 30*, 217–252.

Hutt, M. (2004). Introduction: Monarchy, democracy, and Maoism in Nepal. In M. Hutt (Ed.), *Himalayan people's war: Nepal's Maoist rebellion.* UK: C. Hurst & Co. Ltd..

Lewis, M. P., & Simons, G. F. (2010). *Assessing endangerment: Expanding Fishman's GIDS.* Revue romaine de linguistique 55: 103–120.

Maddox, B. (2003). Language policy, modernist ambivalence and social exclusion: A case study of Rupandehi district in Nepal's terai. *Studies in Nepali History and Society, 8*(2), 205–224.

Malla, K. P. (2015). *From Literature to culture: Selected writings on Nepalese studies, 1980–2010*. Kathmandu: Social Science Baha.

NEPC. (1956). *Education in Nepal*. Report of the Nepal Education Planning Commission, Nepal.

Neupane, D. P. (2010). Nepalko bhasa niti: Bigat bartaman ra aagami sandarva (Nepali language policy: Past, present and future perspectives). *Udvodh, 1*(1), 82–87. Dharan, Sunsari: Nepal University Progressive Teachers' Association, Mahendra Multiple Campus Unit.

Paudel, K. P. (2009). *Ethnicity and language issue in the present context in Nepal*. A paper presented at CET Seminar at Sukuna Multiple Campus, Indrapur, Morang.

Regmi, D. R. (2015). Preserving and promoting the endangered languages of Nepal: Policy, practices and challenges. A paper presented at the International Seminar on Preservation and Promotion of Mother Languages and Multilingualism: Scope of Making IMLI as a Research Hub, organized by International Mother Language Institute (IMLI) 21–22 February, 2015, Dhaka, Bangladesh.

Regmi, D. R. (2017). Convalescing the endangered languages in Nepal: Policy, practice and challenges. *Gipan, 3*(1), 139–149. Kathmandu, Central Department of Linguistics.

Riaz, A., & Basu, S. (2007). *Paradise lost? State failure in Nepal*. UK: Lexington Books.

Scotton, C.-M. (2002). *Linguistics: Bilingual contact encounters and grammatical outcomes*. Oxford: Oxford University Press.

Shah, R. K. (2012). *Code switching in Maithili language (A case study in Siraha district)*. An unpublished MA thesis, Tribhuvan University, Nepal.

Sharma, G. (2000). *Nepalko saikshik itihash (Academic history of Nepal)*. Kathmandu: Lumbini Pustak Bhandar.

Simpson, A. (2007). *Language and National Identity*. United States: Oxford University Press.

Tumbahang, G. B. (2009). Process of democratization and linguistic human rights in Nepal. *Tribhuvan University Journal, XXVI*, 8–16.

Turin, M. (2007). *Linguistic diversity and the preservation of endangered languages: A case study from Nepal*. Kathmandu: ICIMOD.

Yadav. (2015). *Code mixing in Maithili Nepali*. An unpublished MA thesis, Tribhuvan University, Nepal.

Yadav, R. (2013). *Language shift in Maithili speakers: A case study in Kathmandu valley*. An unpublished MA thesis, Tribhuvan University, Nepal.

Yadava, Y. P. (2014). Language use in Nepal. In *Population monograph* (Vol. II, pp. 51–72). Kathmandu: CBS and UNFPA.

Yadava, Y. P., & Turin, M. (2005). Indigenous languages of Nepal: A critical analysis of linguistic situation and contemporary issues. In Y. Prasad Yadava & P. Lal Bajracharya (Eds.), *Indigenous languages of Nepal: Situation, policy planning and coordination*. Kathmandu: NFDIN.

CHAPTER 3

Language Contact in Nepal

3.1 INTRODUCTION

Language contact is a common phenomenon in present-day multilingual Nepal for a number of sociocultural and historical reasons. Historically, Nepal has been ruled by kings and rulers having different languages, cultures and ethnicities. Before the unification movement, parts Nepal were ruled by various small kings such as the Kiratis, Mallas, Khasas and Thakuris, and languages like Maithili, Sanskrit, Newar and Kirati had been in contact with people and rulers. However, after unification, the kings belonging to the Shah dynasty ruled for nearly 300 years and promoted monolingual practice.

Most societies in today's world are multilingual. Language contact occurs when speakers of different languages interact closely; then, it is typical for their languages to influence each other. Language contact can occur at language borders, between commercial division languages or as the result of migration, with an intrusive language acting as either a superstratum or a substratum. It occurs through a variety of processes, including language convergence, borrowing and reflexification. The most common products are pidgins, creoles, code-switching and mixed languages.

During the past few years much has been said and written about language contact and linguistic convergence. Language contact in a particular region may be shaped by many factors, for example, trade, migration, social prestige, dominant vs. minority languages, political superiority and

B. L. Gautam, *Language Contact in Nepal*, https://doi.org/10.1007/978-3-030-68810-3_3

so on. The languages in contact may be related genetically or not. In every case, however, convergence is a linguistic process leading to reduction in linguistic distance between languages in contact. It is simultaneously a linguistic, historical and social phenomenon. It has parallels in other areas of human behavior besides language and has some similarity with the phenomena of acculturation in anthropology and socialization in sociology. In the context of Nepal all the processes are important and play a role in developing language contact activities in some or all Nepalese societies.

3.2   Multilingualism and Language Contact in Nepal

Multilingualism has become a very common phenomenon all over the world. According to *Ethnologue* (2020), there are 7117 languages in the world, far more languages than the number of countries. Of course, the number of speakers of the different languages is haphazardly distributed, meaning that speakers of smaller languages need to speak other languages in their daily life, which creates language contact situations all over the multilingual world.

Language contact in Nepal is very complex comparing most other countries. Before unification movement (1736–1769) Newar, Maithili and Sanskrit were the languages used in Kathmandu Valley and many other ethnic languages such as Tamang, Gurung, Limbu, Rai and Magar prevailed in other parts. After unification, Nepali, Sanskrit and English languages were predominant during the Rana and Panchayat Eras. The greatest impact of multilingualism in Nepal can be observed clearly after the 1990 people's revolution for a multiparty democracy against monarchy. The Nepali-only policy of the absolute monarchy was discarded in favor of an official language policy that recognized Nepal's linguistic diversity (Sonntag 2007: 205). The impact of the Maoist revolution (1996–2006) brought much social and cultural change in Nepalese multilingualism. Many ethnic communities were displaced from their original homelands to the capital city by political pressure and Kathmandu became the center for migrants in terms of education, employment, economic prosperity and political activity.

When languages come into contact in a multilingual situation, we find various causes and consequences. The outcomes of contact may be grouped in three general categories: language shift, language maintenance and language creation. Each setting has certain consequences for the speech community and the languages involved. Shift implies second-language acquisition and results in the loss of a community's native language. Maintenance in contact settings involves second-language acquisition without loss of the native language, and mixing of elements from both languages through borrowing and code-switching. Language creation results in the emergence of novel varieties such as bilingual mixed languages, pidgins and creoles.

Multilingualism has multiple aspects, and researchers in all these areas have different goals when they try to test hypotheses or answer research questions. There are different dimensions: the focus of research may be on individual or social multilingualism, and that it is possible to adopt an atomistic or a holistic perspective. Multilingualism is also extended geographically, and multilingual speakers can be found in all parts of the world. At the societal level, multilingualism can often be found at different levels: in the family, at work and in education. Multilingualism can be developed in early childhood or later on in life, and it can involve an unlimited combination of languages. Research on multilingualism is highly productive, as shown by new proposals, concepts, hypotheses and findings. We need to improve our knowledge of individual and societal multilingualism linked to globalization. The intensification of international contacts, the internationalization of the economy, and the mobility of the population have produced more opportunities to conduct research on multilingualism and have also highlighted the importance of research in this area.

Multilingualism is also a proficiency acquired by an individual, but there tend to be patterns of multilingual proficiency throughout a community. Similar people have similar needs for multilingual proficiency. The study of multilingualism is important for determining the language repertoire of a speech community and also to assess if people may prefer literacy in a language other than their heritage language. Multilingualism may be an indication of a community's shift away from its heritage language to another language. Whereas multilingualism can exist in separate territories, with speakers of different languages living in the same territory not being able to communicate in each other's language (for example, monolingual speakers of English and French in Canada), in situations of plurilingualism, where individuals are using more than one language in their lives, language contact is likely to occur. By language contact, we mean where groups or individuals are using different languages and their use of language is modified as a result. This can occur in several different ways.

English, for example, has borrowed a great deal of vocabulary from French, Latin, Greek, and many other languages in the course of its history without speakers of the different languages having actual contact; book learning by teachers causes them to pass on the new vocabulary to other speakers via literature, religious texts, dictionaries and so on, but many other contact situations have led to language transfer of various types, often so extensive that new contact languages are created.

The discussion of language contact is relevant in the sense that both processes are under way in the speech communities investigated. The following points provide more clarity on this aspect:

1. The first situation involves contact between two language communities who maintain a high degree of social separation. Both language communities retain their native language and only borrow selected items.

2. A high degree of bilingualism between speakers of adjacent languages over a prolonged period of time seems to facilitate the gradual process of language convergence that affects all levels of language, especially the phonology.

3. A third contact-based situation that causes language convergence requires significant intermarriage or other types of family-level intermixing between speech communities, for instance inter-ethnic marriage in Nepal. A large number of the members of one linguistic group may be incorporated into the social structure of another group in various ways: as spouses, as servants or sometimes as refugees. Intermarriage frequently occurs between different speech communities, sometimes voluntarily, sometimes involuntarily on the part of the incoming spouse. When such mixing occurs on a large or prolonged scale, the effect on the language of the incorporating community often goes deeper than the mere borrowing of words. This is especially the case when large groups of women are incorporated into the community from outside, be it as wives or servants charged with helping to raise children. If the newcomers are beyond the age of adolescence, they will necessarily learn the new language with imperfections caused by the interference of their native tongue. If there is a sufficiently large number of these non-native speaking women, they will affect their children's speech, bringing about significant changes in a language. Children can be strongly affected when raised primarily by non-native speakers or by speakers with a

particular dialectal peculiarity. This occurs on a modest scale in Nepalese communities: when a Rai, for example, marries another Rai or other language community, the alternate language is Nepali.

4. Besides causing language convergence of the types just enumerated, language contact can also result in an entire group abruptly abandoning its native speech and adopting a new language. This phenomenon is known as language shift. Language shift happens every time an immigrant learns the native language of the new country and passes it down to children in place of the old-country language. If people undergo language shift at the level of individuals or isolated small groups, then the effects of language shift on the speech community as a whole will be negligible. Generally, the linguistic peculiarities of a single person or a small group of single persons will not be passed down to future generations. In the context of Nepal, young generations, business people and migrant people are shifting towards Nepali and English because of education, urbanization and globalization. A sudden language shift in an entire population, with the accidental language mixing that always occurs in such a situation, can create a new, mixed language, a creole, within the space of a single generation.

The last and most radical form of language change due to language mixing involves a situation when several linguistically diverse groups are confronted with the need to communicate. Today, for political reasons, every country has a national, or official language. In countries where many languages are spoken, very often one dominant language is chosen as a common language. A language used for communication between peoples who speak different languages is called a lingua franca or language of wider communication (LWC). Nepali is a common contact language in Nepal, but the LWC is gradually shifting towards English because of the influence of media, education, trade and globalization. On the other hand, the use of the Hindi language in south Asia and in Nepalese urban areas has been increasing day by day as a new-contact language among young people, businessmen and housewives. Some other factors are discussed below.

3.2.1   Foreign Employment

Following the 1916 agreement between Nepal and British India, Nepalese male youth from the mountain and hill regions started migrating to British

India for employment. This migration took place mainly to obtain military jobs under the British government in India. Initially, the number of migrants was rather small but it gained momentum in later years.

In the middle of the nineteenth century, the British took territorial control of Darjeeling in India from the king of Sikkim. Many of them chose to settle in Darjeeling, a hilly location, due to its temperate climate, a contrast to the excessively hot weather in Calcutta. They later developed Darjeeling as a tea-growing area, as this region had good soil and climate for tea, and people from eastern Nepal were put to work on the tea plantations. The majority of the migrant workers were from the Mongoloid Tibetan-Burman ethnic groups. They suffered hardship due to social discrimination, and linguistic, political, social and economic domination by the "high caste" Tagadhari[1] viz Brahmins and Chetris (Pradhan 1991).

It was Sir David Ochterlony's idea to recruit the Nepalese into the British army, influenced by the bravery of Nepali soldiers in the Anglo-Nepal war (Singh 2009). Thus began the tradition of Nepalese joining the Indian and British armies. Whether working on the tea plantations of Darjeeling or in the army in different parts of the world colonized by the British, both of these jobs were very significant not only in terms of financial gain for the Nepali people, but also as a facilitating factor for Nepali–English language contact.

Some of the Nepali people involved in private foreign employment in various parts of India remained abroad, notably in some parts of India, while others returned to their original home areas. The latter group brought with them some English, words such as *style, cup, ribbon, muffler, suit pant, boot, tyam* (a form of the word "time") etc. The use of English words was not limited to rural areas: language contact was actually more widespread in urban centers.

Those people who were in the Gorkha (Gurkha) regiment had a unique prestige in their home villages. After completing their services in the army, they returned home with different military ranks, such as *sergeant, major* and *captain*. These ex-Gurkhas were valued in their villages and referred to by their previous ranks in the army. The officers had good command of English. Their children were also taught abroad in English-medium schools and colleges. This group of people was the first to speak English language in Nepal, and contributed to raising the status of English. The contact between the Nepali language and the English language has furthermore been strengthened by the establishment of various foreign development agencies across the country.

3.2.2   Media and Music

Media and music are the most influential factors in language contact and shift in the present day. According to Jha (1989), the national radio stations in Kathmandu broadcast predominantly Nepali-language programs, allocating only 11.23% of total transmission time for English news (as cited in Eagle 2000: 43). In addition to this, there was a music program entitled *Music mania* hosted by Harish Chanda, alias Michael Chanda, that played English-language pop songs which contributed to introducing English to Nepalese people.

When Nepal entered fully into the wider world, particularly after the 1990 democratic movement, communication with the outside the world leapt forward. English and Hindi immediately became the languages of entertainment in media and music related communication along with Nepali. A large number of private FM stations have subsequently been set up. Their number is increasing year by year, covering almost all parts of the country. According to Rana (2008: 92), the announcers use approximately 75% English and 25% Nepali. These broadcast media are also helping the English language to move forward in parallel with the Nepali language, thereby increasing Nepali–English bilingualism. As Eagle (2000: 42) says, Nepal is moving towards modernization because of development and media impact. Nepali and English are now the two most important languages in the media, with Hindi occupying third place, particularly in popular music and film.

Foreign TV channels telecasting in English are becoming very popular among the Nepali younger generations. Likewise, the growing use of new technology among Nepalese of all age groups has become a contributing factor in bringing the Nepali language in contact with English. Most music videos and audio files are available in English which is creating contact with the English language to people of all levels and literacy.

3.2.3   Travel and Tourism

Nepal is not only linguistically and culturally diverse, but also varied ecologically and geographically. Due to its diversity in geography and its rich and unique climate, Nepal has a wide range of plant and animal species; it is famous for its flora and fauna. It has the world's highest peak, *Sagarmatha* (Mount Everest), summoning visitors from across the world to climb it. Every year thousands of people from around the world visit Nepal; some of them are on holiday, while some of them come to study the languages and cultures of the people and the country's natural resources. For all of these visitors, whatever their national languages are, English plays a significant role as a medium of communication, from booking tickets and hotels to arranging travel and trekking during their stay in Nepal. Hindi language is widely used in travel and tourism in addition to English.

All stakeholders associated with the travel and tourism industry, such as hotel, restaurant and trekking entrepreneurs, must have knowledge of English in order to communicate with tourists. Not all people involved in this business are highly educated: some are illiterate and run small lodges and restaurants on the trekking routes. They have not developed their foreign language skills formally, but through direct contact with foreigners. Thus, travel and tourism has provided the English language with a channel to make its way to the Nepali people, developing an English-speaking community among them. Further, Nepal has recently become a center for religious excursions by Indian tourists in which Hindi has become the main medium of communication. Tourists visiting Pashupati, Lumbini, Muktinath and many other beautiful places need tour guides who can speak both English and Hindi.

3.2.4   Urbanization and Globalization

Several factors have contributed to the current prominence of multilingualism. Among them, globalization, transnational mobility of the population, and the spread of new technologies are highly influential in different political, social, and educational contexts. Aronin and Singleton (2008) compared the features of historical and contemporary multilingualism. They reported seven distinctions between urbanization and globalization. These distinctions can be clustered into following three main areas:

1. Geographical: In comparison with the past, multilingualism is not limited to geographically close languages or to specific border areas or trade routes. It is a more global phenomenon spread over different parts of the world. The use of English and Hindi in Nepal is an example of this.
2. Social: Multilingualism is no longer associated with specific social strata, professions or rituals. It is increasingly spread across different social classes, professions and sociocultural activities.

3. Medium: In the past, multilingual communication was often limited to writing, and mail was slow. In the twenty-first century, thanks to the internet, multilingual communication has become multimodal and instantaneous.

Globalization has increased the value of multilingualism. Speaking different languages has an added value. As Edwards (2004) pointed out, speaking English can be necessary, but the ability to speak other languages none the less ensures a competitive edge (p. 164). English is the most widely used language in the Internet, however the percentage of Internet users of English has decreased from 51.3% in 2000 to 25.9% in 2020. The second most used language in 2020, was Chinese with 19.4% in total, and third was Spanish with 7.9%. Many other languages are used as well. In the Nepalese context, people without multilingual ability are like a monolingual of 50 years ago. Another important factor for multilingualism is education and privatization where Nepalese students are taught in English-medium classes; the result is clear. Given its growing importance in modern society, multilingualism has attracted increasing attention in various field of social research, as can be seen in the titles of journals, articles, books and academic conferences that use the term "multilingualism."

In recent times, the linguistic dynamic of Nepal has been affected by various other factors. The earthquake of 2015 devastated Ghale village in Gorkha and many Thangmi residential areas in Dolakha. These two speech communities had to leave their original places and started to live in Kathmandu, Chitwan, Pokhara, Charikot or Manthali. The displacement of these two ethnic communities threatens language death because the migrants have to speak the Nepali language for communication in their new locations. So the language contact and multilingualism that naturally developed among Ghale and Thanmi people led to language shift and possible language death. Similarly, the COVID-19 pandemic has also changed the attitudes of language users in the context of Nepal. Most of the terminologies related to COVID-19 and its treatment have not been translated into Nepali and other ethnic languages. As a result, English words like PCR, SARS Virus, Negative, Positive, Quarantine, Home isolation and so on are now widely used and have common currency in Nepal.

3.3   MULTILINGUALISM AND (UN)DEMOCRATIC PRACTICES IN NEPAL

Nepal's multilingualism and linguistic diversity has been connected with a history of various (un)democratic practices. In Nepal, diversity was promoted by democracy through policy provisions, especially after the promulgation of the 1990 Constitution of Nepal following the Nepali-only monolingual policy of the absolute monarchy (the Panchayat regime). The basic right of the use of indigenous languages was assured in the constitution, as were other educational provisions as outcomes of the democratic political turn. The changes in the policy provisions provided opportunities for linguists, language rights activists and advocacy groups/individuals to explore languages and cultures.

Nepal's multilingualism and democratic practices can be divided into three major periods.

3.3.1   *The Ancient Period (Prehistoric to 1769 AD)*

The ancient period of Nepalese history begins with the kings of *Gopal* (cow-herders) and *Mahispal* (buffalo-herders) dynasties. Likewise, the *Kiranti* and *Lichchhabi* dynasties appeared in the first phase and the *Mallas* ruled the second and final phase of the ancient period of Nepalese history. The term "Nepal" is used here for Kathmandu Valley and surrounding areas. Moreover, there were also some small kingdoms of Aryan and Mongolian tribes in other parts of Nepal known as *Baaise* (Twenty-two States) and *Chaubise* (Twenty-four States), and many kingdoms in the Terai region. During this period Sanskrit, Newar and Maithili languages were used in the Nepal valley, and other languages such as Kiranti, Khas Nepali, Magar and Gurung were used in other parts of present-day Nepal.

3.3.2   *The Medieval Period (1769–1951 AD)*

The medieval period of Nepalese history begins with the unification movement of Prithvi Narayan Shaha, a king from Gorkha. He annexed the kingdoms of Nepal Valley (Kathmandu, Patan and Bhaktapur) and further expanded far and wide. The campaign was continued by his successors in a period known as Shaha Rule and the Gorkha kingdom reached the Tibetan plateau in the north, Gangas in the south, Kangada in the west and Tista in the east. Later, the British Empire in India extended northwards to include Nepal's western territory, leaving the present-day Nepal as a British protected state after the Sugauli Treaty in 1816. During the Shaha rule (1769–1846), we do not find any clear language policy or democratic practices. However, the Sanskrit language was promoted as the vernacular of literary and religious works and Khasa bhasa (Nepali language) became the language of law, administration and education.

Janga Bahadur Rana came into power after the Kot Massacre and made the Shah king unofficially his prisoner. Since Ranas belong to the Khas community and are close relatives of the Shaha kings, they continued a Shaha monarchy on the throne, so that linguistically, they continued and strengthened the supremacy of Sanskrit and Khasa (Nepali) in religion and culture. The outline of the autocratic Rana regime depicts a ban on education as a whole and the domination of marginalized languages other than Nepali. The establishment of Gorkha Bhasa Prakasani Samiti (1913), later named Nepali Bhasa Prakasani Samiti (1933) emphasized Nepali languages and ignored other spoken languages of Nepal. Finally, Nepali language was declared the only official language of Nepal by the first constitution of Nepal (GON Act, Article 44, 1948). Basically, Nepali and Sanskrit languages were highlighted and English language education started in Durbar High school only after Janga Bahadur Rana (a powerful Rana prime minister) visited England.

3.3.3   The Modern Period (1951–)

The modern history of Nepal begins with the end of Rana rule in Nepal and the beginning of democracy under a constitutional monarchy. Political parties like Praja Parisad, Nepali Democracy Congress, Nepali National Congress and the Communist Party of Nepal came into existence when King Tribhuvan declared an interim constitution in 1951.The first census was launched in 1952/1954 which officially accepted 44 languages in the country. A national education commission was launched in 1965. At the meantime, the Hindi and Newar languages occupied space in Radio Nepal for news and a limited number of programs.

The Panchayat regime started in 1960 when King Mahendra closed down the elected government and started party-less system. He launched the Panchyat constitution in 1962 in which *one country, one king, one language, one costume* became the ruling slogan and marginalized languages were virtually ignored. This was a golden period for Nepali language and literature: multilingualism was hardly practiced in academia and administration. Multilingualism persisted among the minority language communities despite the compulsion of learning Nepali from the first grade in school.

The political change of 1990 established multi-party democracy and constitutional monarchy in Nepal. The 1990 Constitution of the kingdom of Nepal was launched, which brought about significant change in the country including the recognition of real multilingualism and diversity in various aspects of Nepalese society. The censuses of 1991 and 2001 numbered the languages spoken in Nepal as 32 to 92 respectively. Many news and other programs were launched in one and half dozen languages on Radio Nepal and Nepal television. This led to significant changes in Nepalese society because of the new freedom and strengthened consciousness among the minority-language speaking communities. People started to use and speak their languages outside their family and communities as a part of ethnic and communal solidarity, which increased motivation of language contact and resultant shift.

The Maoist movement (1996–2006) brought many changes in Nepalese multilingualism and language contact politics. This political movement lasted for about a decade and established radical change in diversity and sociocultural activities. People began to migrate to the cities from the villages for employment, education and security. Every city of Nepal became multilingual and diversified. Janaaandolan II ended the monarchy and established federal democratic government in Nepal based on the 2007 Interim Constitution, which recognized all the languages spoken in Nepal as national languages. Constitutional Assembly (CA) members were allowed to take the oath in their mother tongue.

The CA promulgated a new Constitution of Nepal in 2015, based on the 2007 Interim Constitution and many of its articles are now being implemented within the new arrangement of federal states in Nepal. The provision of establishing a Language Commission in Article 287 of the Constitution is one of the most important landmarks in the history preserving and promoting the languages of Nepal. This shows that the democratic political system with its liberal economy has embraced linguistic diversity as a resource, as a result of which the multilingual identity of Nepalese society is officially recognized. However, it has been widely agreed that multilingualism and variability are constitutive of human existence, and we engage in dynamic dialogic interaction to construct our identity based on our diversity (Agnihotri 2017).

3.4   URBANIZATION AND LANGUAGE CONTACT IN NEPAL

The major impact of language contact in Nepal is seen in communication and urbanization. Millions of Nepalese migrated to their nearest cities for employment and better education. Increasing urbanization is mostly the result of foreign employment in the context of Nepal. If we examine Kathmandu over three decades we can observe the effect of migration and urbanization. The Newar inhabitants and are now in the minority, Kathmandu has become a cosmopolitan capital city. Though it has a long religious, cultural and political history, the major population of Kathmandu city is now dominated by different language speakers who migrated from various parts of the country. Nepali is the official language as well as the lingua franca in Kathmandu, though Newar is the dominant language in Kathmandu, used mainly by Newar ethnic communities in their cultural, social and religious activities. Kathmandu has become a multilingual city where we find people speaking at least three or more languages. The term "urbanization" in the Nepalese context means that a large number of other-language speaking peoples like Indo Aryan (such as Maithili, Bhojpuri and Tharu) and Tibeto-Burman (such as Sherpa, Tamang, Gurung, Rai and Limbu) have been migrating in the capital city day by day especially after the political revolution of the 1990s (Gautam 2012). The local people of Kathmandu Valley—Newar speakers and migrants having their own mother tongues such as Gurung, Magar, Limbu, Sherpa and Maithili display and adopt different language ideologies that best reflect their own interests. Nevertheless, ideological change does occur, and the investigations reveal at least the potential for support for a broader kind of multilingualism within the valley, taking into account not only the officially supported languages like Nepali and English, but also the wider range of languages spoken. Different languages are in use for different domains among various speech communities residing in Kathmandu and many other city areas of Nepal such as Pokhara, Dharan, Nepalgunj, Surkhet and Birgunj. Such pattern of language use is constrained by the attitudes of the speech communities. The attitude towards the contact and shift of different languages is governed by different language ideologies. Changes in the current sociolinguistic situation, due in large part to urbanization and internal migration, have debatably given rise to competing language ideologies in Kathmandu Valley, for instance native like Newar and migrant like Sherpa, Limbu, Gurung and Maithili. Comprehensive study also highlights the existing political, social and economic factors that contribute to language use and the attitudes of speakers (Gautam 2020).

3.5   LANGUAGE CONTACT AND CHANGE

Language contact has become the center of attraction for many scholars, who describe it as a phenomenon where two or more different languages come into contact within the same speech community. Weinrich (1953: 1–4) defines language contact as the alternate use of two or more languages by the same individual, and identifies the need for an examination of both psychological and sociocultural factors to clearly understand the behavior of languages in a contact situation. Various other studies on language contact have posited different points of view. In this regard, Thomason (2001: 62) defines contact-induced change as any linguistic change that would have been less likely to occur outside a particular contact situation, that is change due at least in part to language contact. Thomason's broad definition includes not only the changes that emerge as a result of properties being directly imported from one language into another (such as morphemes, syntactic patterns or both) but also changes that take place, especially in dying languages, as a result of speakers shifting to other languages, though such changes may not be direct imports from the dominant language. The third type of change discussed in Thomason (2001) encompasses subsequent changes that take place in a receiving language (RL) as a result of an earlier direct transfer of properties from a source language (SL) into the RL. This definition does not rule out changes that emerge from multiple causation, those that result from the combination of both external and internal causes in the language. Even though many scholars today agree that change is the most frequent outcome of contact (Poplack and Levey 2010), within language contact studies there is no clear consensus on how to ascertain and classify the outcomes that occur as a result of contact. However, language contact can be described as the interactions of different cultures resulting from several constituents such as colonization, migration, urbanization and modernization. In the context of Nepal, language contact has caused significant changes in all aspects of society and people, including communication, education and styles. Nepal's language contact is influenced by sociolinguistic features rather than historical relationships among the languages. Hence, globalization and its impacts are the main causes of increasing language contact activity in Nepal.

3.6   LANGUAGE IDEOLOGY AND ATTITUDES

It is generally agreed that among all of the factors that promote or prevent language shift, the most important is the value assigned to a language by the speakers themselves. Perhaps it goes without saying but it is worth repeating that, as Grenoble and Whaley (1998: 24) write, "the subjective attitudes of a speech community towards its own and other languages are paramount for predicting language shift." It is certainly not always the case that speakers explicitly assign a value to a language. However, whether a language is explicitly valued or not there must be a desire on the part of speakers to speak it. In some cases, this is explained as a language holding covert prestige in the community as a marker of community identity; in others it may simply be explained as a language retaining communicative usefulness in the community. Although the latter is sometimes glossed over, the former clearly falls under the umbrella of individual and community language ideology. Language contact and shift in Nepal has been slightly influenced by neoliberal ideology which is the symbol of modernization and development in the present globalized world.

As Woolard (1998) points out in her introduction to a volume dedicated to the study of language ideology, there is more than one definition of what the study of language ideology, linguistic ideology or ideologies of language might be. But a working definition of language ideology comes from Silverstein (1979: 193), who writes that language ideologies are "any set(s) of beliefs about language articulated by the users as a rationalization or justification of perceived language structure and use." Within the study of language ideology, work has focused on speaker attitudes toward languages or language varieties in multilingual and multidialectal communities, with an underlying assumption that language loyalty is crucial for language maintenance, and for the maintenance of indigenous minority languages in particular. The theoretical approach guiding the research questions and goals of this study are on the notion of language ideologies. In the context of Nepal, looking at the language ideology across the ethnic communities, Sherpas show more loyalty to English and Nepali rather than their mother tongue because they are very much influenced by trekking and foreign employment and tourism (Gautam 2020). On the other hand, the Newars of Kathmandu Valley are more conscious of their mother tongue and they show high solidarity in speaking Newar in their religious and cultural activities. In contrast to Newar and Sherpa, Maithili speakers in Nepal show a greater influence of Hindi language in their educated communities rather than Nepali and English. Every description of language is an ideological umbrella of language ideologies which encourage us to study neglected topics, such as cultural conceptions of the role of language in social life, the role and character of meta-language, and the connection of language choice to commonsense activities as well as the linkage of language and identity.

3.7   Language Contact Studies in Nepal

In the past, the study of language contact itself was a part of sociolinguistic study. There has been much research in various areas of south Asia and Nepal, some of which is summarized below.

Bendix (1974) discusses the various aspects of Nepali and Newar verb tenses in his research during 1965–1966 among various Indo-Aryan and Tibeto-Burman language contacts. He describes the various uses and aspects of Nepali and Newar and their comparison in morphological, syntactic and semantic aspects. He discusses the various examples of linguistic convergence while justifying the language contact between two major families i.e. TB and IA along with some real linguistic features. This preliminary study illustrates the historical contact and relation among the languages of this region.

Turner (1985a) discusses the various aspects of Nepali infinitives based on the tales in Nepali published by the Gorkha Press, Banaras. He uses his personal experience and the stories told by Gorkhas in various periods which show aspects of language contact over the ages. Turner studied and translated the "Birsikka" text in order to find out the infinitive forms viz. -nu, -na, and ne. In another article, Turner (1985b) discusses language contact situations during the First World War (1914–1918) between Gurkha battalions and Scots and Englishmen in various places like Gaza, Jerusalem and France. Turner translated and analyzed the war songs composed by Gurkhas related to a bomb accident, capturing prisoners, winning the war and so on, and described various language contacts featured between Hindi, English and Nepali. The translated songs are the best examples of the language contact situation of that time.

Genetti (1999) presents a quantitative study of gender and number agreement in Nepali which indicates that the prescriptive pattern is vigorous only in formal and written Nepali. Various spoken narratives she has collected so far show less agreement than written Nepali, while in conversation the agreement is quite scarce. Variation in the percentages of agreement across speakers suggests that various sociolinguistic factors are involved in making the difference between the two varieties. She has also presented the data from the two earlier times where *gayechha* suggests that this variation is not recent symbolic of change in progress, but is a constant feature of Nepali grammar. So, the possible motivations for this stable variation include internal markedness considerations and external language contact with speakers of Tibeto-Burman languages in Nepal. The pressures for the loss of agreement are counterbalanced by the conventional influence of the writing system. However, this study motivates various other factors in language contact and change.

Noonan (2003) describes the various language contact situations among the speakers of major language families in his long article "Recent Language Contact in the Nepal Himalaya." He presents various language contact data on 16 Tibeto-Burman languages of Nepal and their language contact situation which has various lexical and grammatical borrowing features. He compares these languages with Nepali and predicts the various language endangerment situations. In his article, he presents a truer picture of the actual spoken languages which show greater convergence with Nepali, which has been the national language of Nepal since the unification movement. His article is more focused on historical relations and contacts among the languages of the Himalaya.

Pradhan (2006) presents the results of a case study she conducted among the Newars of Kathmandu Metropolitan City. She collected 100 data, categorizing them into four age groups: 320, 21–40, 41–60, and above 60. She studied language shift due to various factors contributing to shift, language attitude of speakers and steps taken for language maintenance. Discussing the factors, she points out the existing social, political and economic factors which contribute to language shift. Nepali's status as the dominant language in the city and the lingua franca of the country, and the changing social, cultural and economic structure of the Newar people motivate them towards Nepali rather than their heritage language.

Noonan (2008) reviews the genetic relations of languages in contact situation in a global context. Discussing language contact and various models, he provides a family tree model, assuming that any set of related languages descends from a single ancestor. Giving the genetic classification of language contact, he looks at borrowing, substratism influence, koineization, creoles and so on in Nepalese and many other contexts.

Hildebrandt (2008) examines contacts effects on Manange (Tibeto-Burman, Nepal), discussing the various language contact situations in the

Manange community. She provides the various structural consequences of contact with Nepali: phonology, nominal system, clause combining, lexicon and numerals. She also reviews various factors of language contact situations, such as a rural system and an urban system based on the data she has collected.

Gautam (2012) provides a brief introduction of contact Nepali in Kathmandu Valley and its then sociolinguistic context. He offers a brief introduction to Kathmandu Valley and its development in historical connection. He points out that ancient Nepal experienced Aryan and Mughal invasions from the Indian subcontinent. The unification movement of Prithvi Narayan Shah and the popularity of Bhanubhakta's Ramayan are the main causes for the development of Nepali as an official as well as a contact language throughout the country, which resulted the language contact situation of Kathmandu Valley and its impacts and influences during the course of time. Among various political changes and revolutions, the 1990s revolution against the Panchayat System established multi-party democracy in the country, which brought new awareness in languages. The 1996 Maoist revolution and the 2006/2007 political revolution induced migration village to city, and city to Kathmandu, because of opportunities in employment and education. Kathmandu Valley became home to a cosmopolitan city because of this migration from different parts of the country. Talking about the various reasons and domains of contact Nepali in Kathmandu Valley, he briefly describes the nature of migration in Indo-Aryan and Tibeto- Burman communities and the effects of language contacts.

Regmi (2013) provides a description and analysis of contact-induced change in Bhujel, a Tibeto Burman language spoken in Nepal. He describes the sociolinguistic situation of Bhujel language including a discussion of the identification of Bhujel language and its comparison with Chepang in phonology, morphology, syntax and lexical level. He also describes the mother tongue proficiency, history of social relations, bilingual ability of Bhujel people among other neighboring ethnic groups such as Nepali, Gurung, Magar and Ghale. In another part of his article, Regmi discusses the linguistic outcomes of the contact in which he describes lexical comparison based on the basic vocabulary (CDL, TU) related to different semantic domains from Nepali to Bhujel. He also discusses the phonological outcomes of Bhujel and Nepali in tonality, vowels, murmur, voicing and stress. He further provides many examples from the Bhujel language which display different contact phenomena. He also attributes language contact to Nepali's influence and dominance in the Bhujel community in different domains.

Dhakal (2014) investigates the impacts of Nepali (IA) on lexical and morph syntactic features of the Baram language (TB). He describes the sociolinguistic setting of Baram and Nepali and some typological similarities between the two languages. He also notes that among 3652 Baram words only 1022 are native; the rest are borrowed from Nepali and that nouns, verbs and adjectives are borrowed more than other word classes. Dhakal also presents the summary of Baram lexicon (native vs borrowed) recorded in Hunter (1978) and Kansakar (2011) of a total of 176 vocabulary items. He also discusses some cases of contact-induced morphological changes in Baram where both languages share plural suffix *–haru* in Nepali and *–ban* in Baram, as well as the numerals and genitive markers in Baram. While reviewing syntax he notes that Baram has borrowed some syntactic constructions like classifiers from Nepali. In certain contexts, native morphology or syntax is employed, whereas in other contexts borrowed morphology or syntactic mechanisms are employed. The native or borrowed morpho-syntactic construction depends on speakers, contexts and discourse topics. He describes comparative markers *bhan-da*, copula ho, relative-correlative, conjunction rƏ, sentence conjunction * Əni* etc. which have been used and shared for long time.

Phyak (2016) presents a detailed theoretical study of language ideologies and multilingual education policies and practices in Nepal in his unpublished PhD dissertation. At the outset he discusses the background, motivation and research problems and questions of the study. He then deals with the theoretical aspects of language ideology and its historical development. More specifically, he discusses decolonizing language ideologies in relation to the multilingual turn in language education and policies. Following this, he focuses on the conceptual framework of the study and engaged language policy. The notions of ideological becoming, ideological clarification, counter-narratives, indigenous praxis, critical language awareness, and language activism, all related to engaged language policy, are also discussed in his study. Phyak critically analyzes Nepal's current language policy discourses and practices. After this, he deals with the impact of nation-state ideology, analyzing how neoliberalism has informed current language policies and practices in education. Finally, engaged ethnography as a research methodology is examined in the dissertation.

Regmi (2017) reviews the vitality of the languages of Nepal and critically evaluates present policy and practice in recuperating the endangered languages of Nepal. He enumerates various challenges and suggests some plans for meeting those challenges in restoring the vitality of Nepal's languages. Nepal followed a language assimilation policy for more than one and a half centuries. Even after the restoration of democracy, Nepal lacked a clear vision in framing a multilingual language policy. More than 56% of the languages in Nepal are facing different levels of language endangerment. Perfunctory attempts made by government and non-government agencies have not been goal-oriented. Day-by-day, minority speech communities are gradually shifting to Nepali, the language of the wider communication. Their life-crucial indigenous knowledge is dying out as they are gradually assimilated to the mainstream culture. In order to address all these problems Nepal requires a real multilingual language policy which can encourage speech communities to bring their languages into speaking, broaden the domains of language use and ensure quality basic education in the mother tongue. While presenting various data in language vitality and constitutional provisions, Regmi critically analyzes the overall scenario of language policy and planning in Nepal. He outlines the situation of vitality of languages of Nepal in which he tries to evaluate the language policy and planning in Nepal. He also examines the practice of language preservation and the challenges for recuperating the endangered languages of Nepal. Finally, he suggests some strategies for revitalizing/ convalescing them.

Gautam (2017) explores the status of language use and attitude within the Sherpa-speaking community in Kathmandu Valley, the multilingual capital city of Nepal. The study focuses on language contact situations in different domains: social, cultural, personal and official as well as media-related activities where the informants were found to use different languages along with the use of their own mother tongue. This study was based on 45 questionnaires which were administered to different informants, and the data obtained were analyzed taking into account different parameters such as age, gender, profession and location. This research is connected with the sociopolitical factors/ variables where different language communities/ speakers share different contexts and situations. So, in Kathmandu Valley, multilingualism has become an obligatory feature of life in the city. Existing political, social and economic factors contribute to language use and attitude. Nepali, the dominant language in the capital city, has come to be the lingua franca of the country; English, being the international language for various purposes, is becoming more valuable and influential in the Sherpa community which, in turn, indicates language shift and endangerment.

Gautam (2018a) in his article "Language Shift in Sherpa" tries to identify the various aspects of language change and shifts among Sherpa, the ethnic immigrant language community living in Kathmandu Valley. The article focuses on research based on various language contact situations in different domains: social, cultural, religious, personal, and official as well as media-related activities where the informants are asked to use the different languages such as Nepali, English and Hindi, rather than their mother tongue. Gautam briefly introduces Sherpa language and its status with his method of research. He also examines the use of Nepali language and finds that Nepali is predominantly used in social, official, ceremonial and media-related activities whereas the mother tongue, Sherpa, is restricted to religious and cultural activities. The influence of English is much higher than Hindi, which indicates that Sherpa are motivated towards globalization and Western traditions. Sherpa have been directly involved in tourism and trekking and the contact with many foreigners motivates them towards English rather than other languages.

Gautam (2018b) explores different patterns of language shift in Newar, the ethnic indigenous language community living in Kathmandu Valley. His research focuses on language contact situations in social, cultural, personal and official domains as well as media-related activities where the informants were asked to use different languages along with the use of their own mother tongue, Newar. This socioethnographic research provides some clues as to how the discovery of a minority language triggers changes in representations and attitudes. The article deals with the various aspects of language shift in Newar, based on the study of Kathmandu Valley. It deals with the introduction of Newari language and its profile in Kathmandu Valley. Further, it describes the methodology used in this study before briefly discussing patterns of language shift and then language contact and intergenerational shift. In the following section he presents the causes and impacts of language shift, based on data accumulated through various questionnaires, FGD and interviews which show that mother tongue is heavily used in cultural and religious activities, that Nepali is dominantly used in social, official, ceremonial and media-related activities and English and Hindi are used in media, ceremonial and official activities. The influence of English is much higher than Hindi among Newar people, which indicates the influence of globalization and western traditions. Newars have been directly involved in official and academic activities as well as in tourism, which motivates them to communicate with many foreigners in English and Nepali rather than other languages. A shift in a language often brings about a shift in identity and there may be resistance to adopting a new language. The new language and the new identity may be actively promoted or persuaded. Newar living in the capital city have been influenced directly and indirectly by globalization and international linkage and communication. Moreover, they have been involved in various social, cultural and ceremonial activities with the new mixed society which motivates them to shift into new target languages from the ancestral source language.

Thapa et al. (2018) carried out a general study of language shift in Nepal. Their study concentrates on themes emerging from fieldwork data. Three major themes—the trend of language shift focusing on Dotyali, Jumli, Maithili, Tharu, Newar and Nepali referencing different domains of activities and intergenerational interactions—are developed. The study explores the causes and impacts of language shift and goes on to present its major findings and recommendations. Some of the important recommendations from research to policy-level implications include the following: language shift is a natural linguistic phenomenon in the space of language contact which needs to be studied more extensively in the social context; the patterns of language shift vary from one language to another, one geographical location to another and one social situation to another, characterization of which needs to be more specific in terms of language and space; language shift is a cumulative process and can be observed not only in instrumental functions of language use but also at the phonetic/phonemic level, the lexical level, the grammatical level and the semantic level; linguistic study as such needs to be launched extensively. Finally, so that the government of Nepal should promote mother-tongue education in a framework of multilingual education, mother tongue education and inclusive education have been emphasized by the Constitution of Nepal.

Gautam (2020) provides a comprehensive details of language contact study in Kathmandu Valley. He focuses on the patterns of language use and attitudes among three language-speaking communities living in Kathmandu Valley, the capital of Nepal. He has tactfully selected three languages—Sherpa, Maithili and Newar—for which he attempts to show the impact of migration from different geographical locations. Sherpa are the migrants from mountainous and upper hilly regions, whereas Maithilis are the migrants from the plains of the Terai region and the Newars are the ethnic inhabitants of the Kathmandu Valley. This study presents the language contact situation of Kathmandu Valley from the perspective of language ideology with reference to patterns of language use and attitudes in the three languages. It shows how Newar speakers demonstrate language ideologies different from Sherpa and Maithili speakers, who are migrants. It also explores the causes and impacts of language contact among the inhabitants of the location. It also sketches out the multilingual context of Nepal in general, focusing on language contact situations of the three selected language-speaking communities from various ideological perspectives. This comprehensive study also highlights the existing political, social and economic factors which contribute to language and the attitudes of speakers. Moreover, it presents a general sketch of language contact in Kathmandu Valley that deals with various aspects of language contact situations in newly migrated cities in different parts of the world.

*　*　*

By observing and analyzing the available literature in language contact studies, it has become clear that this area of sociolinguistic study has not been done carefully in order to explore further avenues in the Nepalese context. However, the reviews of literature given above are directly and indirectly connected to developing the theoretical and methodological background of studies which will be discussed in further chapters.

3.8 SUMMARY

This chapter briefly summarizes the language contact situation of Nepal connecting with linguistic diversity and multilingualism. It also describes different aspects and the causes of language contact in Nepalese context. It briefly introduces language politics in Nepal connecting with various (un)democratic practices in different periods of the country's history. Nepal is a country where we see contact among languages for long time as a result of politics, religion and cultural amalgamation. One of the most important parts of this chapter is a detailed review of language contact studies of Nepal from various perspectives. These studies on language attitude, ideology and change provide reference and feedback for further studies.

NOTE

1. A group of people in the Hindu religion who wear *Janai* (Holy thread).

BIBLIOGRAPHY

Agnihotri, R. K. (2017). Identity and multilinguality: The case of India. In *Language policy, culture, and identity in Asian contexts* (pp. 185–204). London: Routledge. https://doi.org/10.4324/978135092034.

Aronin, L., & Singleton, D. (2008). Multilingualism as a new linguistic dispensation. *International Journal of Multilingualism, 5*(1), 1–16.

Bendix, H. E. (1974). Indo Aryan and Tibeto-Burman contact: As seen through Newari and Nepali verb tenses. *International Journal of Dravidian Linguistics,* III(I), India.

Dhakal, D. N. (2014). Contact induced change in Baram. *North East Indian linguistics, 6,* 167–190. Canberra: Australian National University.

Eagle, S. (2000). The language situation in Nepal. In R. B. Baldauf & R. B. Kaplan (Eds.), *Language Planning in Nepal, Taiwan and Sweden* (pp. 170–225). Sydney: Multilingual Matters Ltd.

Edwards, V. (2004). *Multilingualism in the English speaking world: Pedigree of nations.* Oxford: Wiley-Blackwell.

Gautam, B. L. (2012). Contact Nepali in Kathmandu valley: Convergence between TB & IA languages. *Nepalese Linguistics, 27,* 38–42.

Gautam, B. L. (2017). Language use and attitude among the Sherpa speaking community in Kathmandu valley. *Gipan, 3*(2), 26–37. Kathmandu, Central Department of linguistics, TU.

Gautam, B. L. (2018a). Language shift in Newar: A case study in the Kathmandu valley. *Nepalese Linguistics, 33*(1), 33–42.

Gautam, B. L. (2018b). Language shift in Sherpa. *Interdisciplinary Journal of Linguistics (IJL), 11,* 119–129. University of Kashmir, India.

Gautam, B. L. (2020). *Language contact in Kathmandu.* An unpublished PhD dissertation, Tribhuvan University, Kathmandu.

Genetti, C. (1999). Variation in the agreement in the Nepali finite verb. In Y. Yadava & W. W. Glover (Eds.), *Topics in Nepalese linguistics* (pp. 542–556). Kathmandu: Royal Nepal Academy.

Grenoble, L. A., & Whaley, L. J. (1998). Toward a typology of language endangerment. In L. A. Grenoble & L. J. Whaley (Eds.), *Endangered languages: Language loss and community response.* New York: Cambridge University Press.

Hildebrandt, A. K. (2008). *How low can you Go?* Contact in Manange (Sino-Tibetan, Nepal) http://www.google.com.

Hunter, W. W. (1978). *A comparative dictionary of the languages of India and high Asia*. New Delhi: Cosmo Publications.

Jha, U. (1989). *Maithili vayakaran aa aur rachana*. Bharati Bhawan Publishers and Distributors.

Kansakar, T. R. (2011). *A sociolinguistic survey of Newar language*. A report submitted to Linguistic Survey of Nepal, Central Department of Linguistics, Kathmandu.

Noonan. (2008). *Genetic classification and language contact*. Retrieved from http/www.google.com.

Noonan, M. (2003). Recent language contact in the Nepal Himalaya. In D. Bradley, R. Lapolla, B. Michailovsky, & G. Thurgood (Eds.), *Language variation: Papers on variation and change in the Sinosphere and in the Indosphere in Honour of James A Matisoff* (pp. 65–88). Canberra: Pacific Linguistics.

Phyak, P. (2016). *For our Cho:tlung: Decolonizing language ideologies and (Re) imaging multilingual education policies and practices in Nepal*. Unpublished PhD dissertation, University of Hawai at Manoa.

Poplack, S. & Levey, S. (2010). Contact-induced grammatical change. In Peter Auer & Jürgen Erich Schmidt (Eds.). *Language and Space – An international handbook of linguistic variation: Volume 1 – Theories and methods* (pp. 391–419). Berlin: Mouton de Gruyter.

Pradhan, J. (2006). Language shift in Newar. In *Nepalese linguistics*, Vol. 22. Kathmandu: Linguistic Society of Nepal.

Pradhan, K. (1991). *The Gorkha Conquest: The processes and consequences of the unification of Nepal, with particular reference to eastern Nepal*. Calcutta: Oxford University Press.

Rana, B. K. (2008). Recent change and development in different language communities in Nepal. In J. W. Mohammad (Ed.), *Linguistic dynamism in South Asia*. New Delhi: Gyan Publishing House.

Regmi, D. R. (2013). Contact induced change in Bhujel. *Nepalese Linguistics, 28*, 167–177. Kathmandu, Linguistic Society of Nepal.

Regmi, D. R. (2017). Convalescing the endangered languages in Nepal: Policy, practice and challenges. *Gipan, 3*(1), 139–149. Kathmandu, Central Department of Linguistics.

Silverstein, M. (1979). Language structure and linguistic ideology. In P. R. Clyne, W. F. Hanks, & C. L. Hofbauer (Eds.), *The elements: A para session on linguistic units and levels* (pp. 193–247). Chicago: Chicago Linguistic Society.

Singh, R. K. (2009). *Global Dimensions of Indo-Nepal Political Relations: Post independence*. India: Gyan Publishing House.

Sonntag, K. S. (2007). Change and permanence in language politics in Nepal. In A. B. M. Tsui & J. Tollefson (Eds.), *Language policy, culture, and identity in Asian contexts* (pp. 205–217). Mahwah: Lawrence Erlbaum.

Thapa, R., Luitel, B., Gautam, B. L., & Devkota, K. R. (2018). *Language shift in Nepal: A general study*. A report submitted to Language Commission Nepal, Kathmandu.

Thomason, S. G. (2001). *Language contact: An introduction*. Edinburgh: Edinburgh University Press.

Turner, R. L. (Ed.). (1985a). Indo Aryan linguistics: Collected papers (1912–1972). In *The Infinitive in Nepali* (pp. 76–87). Delhi: Disha Publications.

Turner, R. L. (Ed.). (1985b). Indo Aryan linguistics: Collected papers (1912–1972). In *Further Specimen in Nepali* (pp. 156–172). Delhi: Disha Publications.

Weinrich, U. (1953). *Languages in contact: Findings and problems*. Hague, the Netherlands: Mouton.

Woolard, K. A. (1998). Introduction: Language ideology as a field of inquiry. *Language ideologies: Practice and theory*, ed. by B. B. Schieffelin, K. A. Woolard and P. V. Kroskrity, pp. 3–47. Oxford: Oxford University Press.

Language Contact in Sherpa

4.1 INTRODUCTION

This chapter deals with language contact situations in the Sherpa-speaking community living in Kathmandu Valley. It consists of six sections: Sect. 4.2 introduces the Sherpa people and language, with a brief account of the ethnolinguistic situation in Kathmandu Valley; Sect. 4.3 describes the various patterns of language use in the Sherpa community; Sect. 4.4 covers language contact and intergenerational shift; Sect. 4.5 deals with language attitudes in the Sherpa community; Sect. 4.6 presents an analysis of the causes and impacts of language contact in Sherpa; and Sect. 4.7 summarizes the main findings of the chapter.

4.2 SHERPA PEOPLE AND LANGUAGE

4.2.1 The Sherpa People

The Sherpa people are of Tibetan origin and cultural affinity. They migrated from eastern Tibet in several waves from the sixteenth through the eighteenth centuries, and settled in the present Solukhumbu area of Nepal, south of the Himalayas, near Mt. Jomolangma (Mount Everest). Sherpa are also found in three other regions adjacent to the Khumbu: Shorong (Solu), Pharak and Rolwaling. Sherpa settlements are generally found at elevations between 2000 and 4500 meters above sea level. The

© The Author(s), under exclusive license to Springer Nature Switzerland AG 2021
B. L. Gautam, *Language Contact in Nepal*,
https://doi.org/10.1007/978-3-030-68810-3_4

51

four main Sherpa villages of Khumbu are Nauche (Nep: Namche Bazaar), Khumjung, Khunde and Thame. The others are Tengpoche (Nep: Thyangpoche), Pangpoche, Dingpoche, Pheriche, Lopuche, Gorakshep, Phortse, Gokyo, Dole, Luza, Macharma, Khumjung, Khumde (alt: Khunde), Thamo, Thame and Yilajung (alt: Yulajung). The Sherpa villages of Pharak are Thumbuk, Monzo, Phemkaro, Phakdingma, Chhutrawa, Yulnying, Kusum Tsangka, Nacho Pomdo, Lomzo, Kyongmo, Buwa, Tate, Seogma, Rimejung, Tshermadingma, Lukla and Dungde. There are many more Sherpa settlements in the Shorung (Solu) region: Salleri is particularly populous because of its status as the district administrative center. The other Sherpa settlements in this region are Katidrangka (Nep: Kharikola), Manidingma (Nep: Nunthala), Trakshingtok, Ringmo, Salung, Jung (Nep: Junbesi), Thraktobuk, Changma (Nep: Bhandar), Thodung, Phaplu, Patale, Kyilkording, Gyapzuwa, Gholila, Setra, Sakar, Jalsa, Pang Khongma, Tsatuk, Kyama, Nyimare and Mopung. A substantial number of Sherpa speakers are also found in Sankhuwasabha and Taplejung districts to the east of Solukhumbu and in Dolakha, Sindupalchok and Ramechaap districts to the west of Solukhumbu. There are also some Sherpa speakers in Rasuwa district, which is otherwise predominantly populated by Tamangs.

These days, Kathmandu Valley has become a meeting place for Sherpa speakers from different mountainous regions because of seasonal as well as permanent migration. Some young Sherpa living in Kathmandu or elsewhere outside of the Solukhumbu area no longer speak the mother tongue. Also, members of other ethnic groups with which the Sherpa are in close contact may identify themselves as Sherpa, though they do not speak the language. In recent decades, the Sherpa have become increasingly involved in running tourism businesses such as travel logistics, hotel and lodge operation, trekking, climbing and guiding. Sherpa have also expanded international appreciation for their mountaineering skills, and some of them have become quite famous. The Sherpa practice Vajrayana Buddhism and are followers of the Nyingma School. Table 4.1 presents summary information about the Sherpa population in different censuses.

Table 4.1 shows that the proportion of Sherpas in the population of Nepal has been decreasing if we compare census 1952/1954 to 2011. In the first census, there were 0.85% Sherpa in Nepal but the 2011 census showed that they were only 0.43%. This indicates the language contact and shift impact of Sherpa migration.

Table 4.1 Sherpa population in Nepal, 1952–2011

SN	Census year	Total population	Proportion of total population
1	1952/1954	70,132	0.85%
2	1961	84,229	0.89%
3	1971	79,218	0.69%
4	1981	73,589	0.49%
5	1991	121,819	0.66%
6	2001	129,771	0.57%
7	2011	114,830	0.43%

Source: Census reports of Nepal

4.2.2 The Sherpa Language

The Sherpa language belongs to the Sino-Tibetan family, which has several dialects spoken in different places. These varieties share a common history: it is widely believed that are all derived from Old Tibetan, a language verified at the time of the Tibetan Empire (seventh to ninth centuries). The large linguistic family of Sino-Tibetan, which comprises about 400 languages, includes the Tibeto-Burman family, which in turn includes Sherpa. Although the Tibeto-Burman languages are genetically related, they show wonderful diversity and they sometimes differ entirely in their vocabulary and syntax. This is not at all the case within the Tibetan family, whose languages are closely related and share many common features even when they are not always mutually intelligible. The Tibeto-Burman languages are currently spoken in five countries viz. China, India, Nepal, Bhutan and Pakistan. Languages closely related to Sherpa phonology and vocabulary bear many similarities with the Tö and Tsang dialects of the Ü-Tsang or "Central Tibetan" language, which are spoken on the northern side of Jomolangma (Mount Everest). Some Kham influences can also be identified, as well as a few features shared with Dzongkha and Drenjong, two Tibetic languages spoken south of the Himalayas, predominantly in Bhutan and Sikkim. As far as morphology and syntax are concerned, one may also observe similarities with Tö and Tsang, but Sherpa has undergone its own evolution, especially in terms of verb morphology. The influences of the Tö, Tsang and Kham dialects on Sherpa can be explained by historical factors: The Sherpa migrated from Tibet via Kham (in eastern Tibet) to Tö (in western Tibet) before settling in the present Solukhumbu area.

4.2.3   The Ethno-Linguistic Situation of Sherpa
         in Kathmandu Valley

According to the census report of 2011, the ethnic population of the Sherpa is 112,946. Kathmandu itself has a sizable Sherpa population, while small number of Sherpa communities can be found throughout Nepal, even in the Terai region. Sherpa communities also live in the Indian state of Sikkim and the hill towns of Darjeeling and Kalimpong. Sherpa are relatively new migrants to Kathmandu Valley; in the beginning they were merely seasonal migrants. The 1990 political movement brought a lot of changes to Nepalese societies, cultures and politics. The partyless Panchayat system changed into a multiparty system, and the powerful monarchy became ceremonial, so that the dominated minority groups from all aspects of society flourished automatically, including their languages. On the other hand, people started migrating to the nearest cities and to the capital from the villages because of job and political opportunities and better education. Census 2001 showed that there were 15,537 Sherpa living in Kathmandu Valley whereas the 2011 census recorded 24,778. Migrated Sherpa speak different languages in different domains and for different purposes. Kathmandu being the capital city of Nepal people from different castes, religion and ethnic groups live together and share a common feeling of brotherhood and nationality. The population of Kathmandu Valley is now dominated by different language speakers migrated from various parts of the country, hence Nepali both is the official language and the language for wider communication (LWC). Kathmandu has now become a multilingual city where we find people speaking at least three languages, often more. Because of urbanization, a large number of speakers of other languages, such as Indo-Aryan (Maithili, Bhojpuri, Tharu, etc.) and Tibeto-Burman (Sherpa, Tamang, Gurung, Rai, Limbu etc.) migrate to the capital city day by day especially since the 1990s political revolution. This movement of people offers many possibilities to study language contact and linguistic convergence (Gautam 2012).

Sherpa migrate to the capital city from various hilly and mountainous regions of Nepal, viz. Solukhumbu, Dolakha, Taplejung, Sindhupalchok, Ramechhap and Tehrathum. They settle in different areas of Kathmandu Valley, mainly at Chabahil, Bauddha, Jorpati, Kapan, Mandikhatar and Gongabu. Table 4.2 presents the Sherpa population in Kathmandu Valley at two different census dates.

Table 4.2 Sherpa Population in Kathmandu Valley

SN	Districts	2001			2011			Increment
		Total	Male	Female	Total	Male	Female	
1	Kathmandu	20,133	10,048	10,065	23,460	11,684	11,776	7.6%
2	Lalitpur	748	340	408	1020	481	539	15.38%
3	Bhakatapur	183	91	92	298	149	149	23.90%
	Grand Total	21,064	10,479	11,097	24,748	12,314	12,434	8.04%

Source: CBS (2001a, 2011)

Table 4.2 indicates that the migration of Sherpa in Kathmandu Valley resulted in an increase in Kathmandu of 7.6% in 10 years, of 15.38% in Lalitpur and 23.90% in Bhakatapur district. The average increment is only 8.04%. One interesting feature is that female Sherpa migration is higher than male. Multilingualism and language contact in Kathmandu Valley is very complex compared to contact situations in other places in the world. The reason behind this is the number and range of historical connections of Kathmandu Valley even before the unification movement, for instance during the eras of the Kirat, Lichhabi and Malla kings.

4.3   DOMAINS OF LANGUAGE USE IN SHERPA

This section mainly deals with the trends of language shift, focusing on the diverse domains of language use and attitudes among the Sherpa language speakers living in Kathmandu Valley. The patterns of language shift observed in the Sherpa speech community are discussed in the following sub-sections.

4.3.1   Informal Situations

Informal situations are those situations in which people do various activities without being conscious of or caring about the outer community. Informal situations in this speech community comprise two types of activities: behavioral and personal. They are briefly discussed below.

4.3.1.1 Behavioral Activities

Behavioral activities in this research mean those activities which indicate the different psychological behavior of the informants. Those activities include activities like making friends, different reading and writing activities, making telephone calls, talking with different people, shopping, passing exams and so on. The domains of language use in different behavioral activities are presented in Table 4.3.

Table 4.3 shows that Sherpa use Nepali language rather than their mother tongue and other languages in almost all behavioral activities. The use of Sherpa is highly influential in making friends and making telephone calls while English is used a great deal in reading and writing and in exams. One can quickly notice that the use of Nepali by 100% of respondents in shopping indicates the influence of Nepali language among city-centered Sherpa. The Hindi language is not very important among Sherpa in these activities. Figure 4.1 shows the patterns of language use in different behavioral activities among the Sherpa residing in Kathmandu Valley.

Figure 4.1 shows Sherpa use multiple languages for multiple activities. The frequency of Nepali, Sherpa and English is higher than other languages. This indicates the strong effect of language contact and shift among the Sherpa-speaking community.

Table 4.3 Domains of language use in behavioral activities[1]

Activities	Languages					
	Sherpa	Nepali	English	Hindi	Others	Conditional
Making friends	57.77%	84.44%	28.88%	11.11%	8.88%	6.66%
Shopping	6.66%	100.00%	13.33%	4.44%	4.445	2.22%
Making telephone calls	66.66%	95.55%	20.00%	4.44%	–	–
Talking with workers	20.00%	93.33%	17.77%	4.44%	6.66%	–
Talking with teachers/professors	6.66%	73.33%	28.88%	2.22%	–	2.22%
Talking with academics	11.11%	80.00%	26.66%	2.22%	4.44%	2.22%
Getting a job	2.22%	64.44%	35.55%	–	2.22%	2.22%
Reading and writing	2.22%	77.77%	46.66%	–	4.44%	–
Passing exams	4.44%	55.55%	44.44%	–	–	–

Source: Gautam (2020)

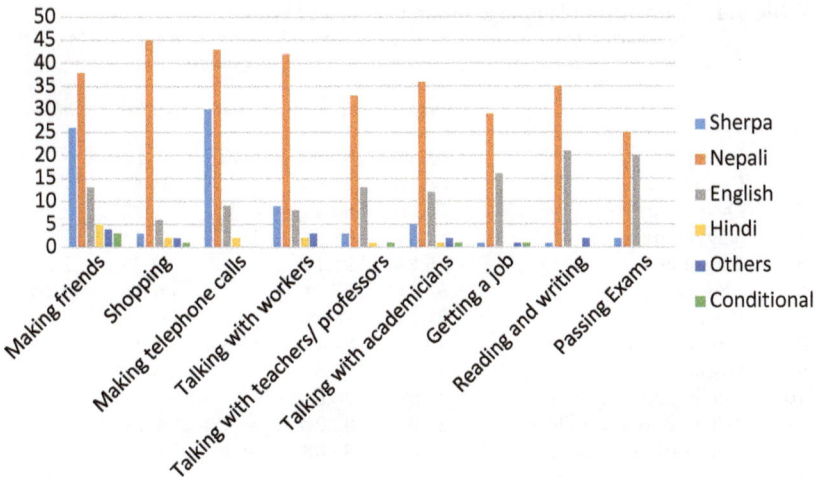

Fig. 4.1 Domains of language use in behavioral activities. (Source: Gautam 2020)

4.3.1.2 Personal Activities

Personal activities in this research mean those activities which are connected to the personal and interpersonal activities of the informants. They include activities such as joking, singing, praying, bargaining, abusing and telling stories.

Table 4.4 shows that Sherpa and Nepali languages are used in most of the domains of personal activities in comparison to Hindi, English and others. The influence of English is much higher than that of Hindi because of education, globalization and tourism connected to Sherpa people. The Sherpa language is used in praying (91%), family gathering (88.8%), quarrelling (77.7%) and many other community-related activities. Nepali is heavily used in such activities as telling stories, community meeting, bargaining and joking, while the use of English and Hindi is limited to joking, singing and counting.

Table 4.4   Domains of language use in personal activities

Domains		Languages				
		Sherpa	*Nepali*	*Hindi*	*English*	*Others*
1.	Joking	68.8%	80.0%	4.4%	2.2%	–
2.	Counting	68.8%	75.5%	–	24.4%	–
3.	Quarreling	77.7%	84.4%	–	2.2%	2.2%
4.	Singing inside	68.8%	48.8%	15.5%	11.1%	–
5.	Bargaining	8.8%	91.1%	–	13.3%	2.2%
6.	Abusing	57.7%	77.7%	–	6.6%	2.2%
7.	Praying	91.1%	8.8%	–	–	6.6%
8.	Singing outside	40.0%	84.4%	15.5%	11.1%	–
9.	Discussing	71.1%	75.5%	–	24.4%	–
10.	Family gathering	88.8%	26.6%	–	–	–
11.	Telling stories to children	20.0%	82.2%	–	4.4%	–
12.	Telling stories to others	20.0%	88.8%	–	4.4%	–
13.	Village/community meeting	71.1%	73.3%	–	–	2.2%

Source: Gautam (2017, 2020)

4.3.2   Formal Situation/Activities

The Sherpa in the Kathmandu valley present an interesting pattern of language use in the domains of official and public domains like office and workplace, political and social gatherings, funfair and public activities, administration and with strangers. Table 4.5 presents the pattern of language use in official and public domains.

Table 4.5 shows the use of multiple languages in multiple activities. Nepali and English are dominant in almost all official and public activities. Sherpa is not very much used in these domains because of its lack of impact. Both Nepali and English are official as well as contact languages for national and international relations. The domains of language use in the Sherpa community in the Kathmandu Valley are presented in Fig. 4.2.

Figure 4.2 indicates the effects of language contact and shift among the Sherpa living in Kathmandu Valley; Nepali and English is very much more influential than Sherpa and Hindi.

4.3.3   Religious and Cultural Activities

Religious and cultural activities are those which are observed and performed by Sherpa people in order to show and preserve their religious and

Table 4.5 Domains of language use in formal situations

Situations		Language use			
		Sherpa	Nepali	English	Hindi
1.	Office/Workplace	7(15.5%)	35(7.8%)	15(33.3%)	8(17.8%)
2.	Political/Social gathering	1(2.2%)	33(7.3%)	5(11.1%)	–
3.	Public activities/Funfair	10(22.22%)	32(7.1%)	6(12.33%)	2(4.4%)
4.	Administration	–	42(93.3%)	4(8.9%)	–
5.	Strangers	1(2.22%)	43(95.5%)	7(15.5%)	2(4.4%)

Source: Gautam (2017, 2020)

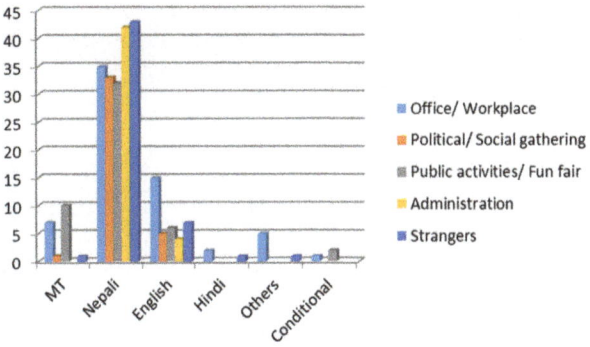

Fig. 4.2 Domains of language use in official and public activities. (Source: Gautam 2020)

cultural values. These activities include birth ceremonies, marriage ceremonies and religious and cultural festivals. The Sherpa community living in the Kathmandu Valley displays a different pattern of the use of mother tongue and Nepali in different activities related to culture and religion. Table 4.6 presents the pattern of language use in different cultural and religious festivals and ceremonies.

Table 4.6 shows that Sherpa mainly use their mother tongue in religious and cultural activities; in religious festivals like Lohsar, where they enjoy musical and cultural nourishment. In this community, Nepali is noticeably used in cultural programs and festivals. English is used in religious festivals, but not to a significant extent. This pattern of language use in the Sherpa community in the Kathmandu valley is illustrated in Fig. 4.3.

Table 4.6 Domains of language use in cultural and religious activities

	Domains	Languages		
		Sherpa	*Nepali*	*English*
1.	Religious festivals	44 (97.8%)	4 (8.9%)	2 (4.4%)
2.	Cultural programs	44 (97.8%)	15 (33.3%)	–
3.	Death ceremonies	45 (100.0%)	7 (15.5%)	–
4.	Marriage ceremonies	45 (100.0%)	8 (17.8%)	–
5.	Birth ceremonies	45 (100.0%)	7 (15.5%)	–
6.	Cultural festivals	41 (91.1%)	12 (26.7%)	–

Source: Gautam (2017, 2020)

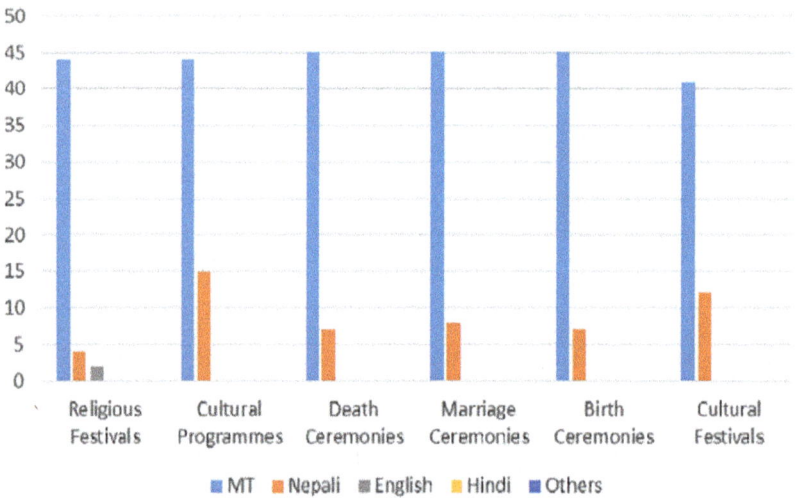

Fig. 4.3 Language use in religious and cultural activities. (Source: Gautam 2020)

Figure 4.3 shows the high frequency of Sherpa language and its use in various religious and cultural activities. We can observe that shifting to Nepali language is relatively rapid in cultural programs and festivals compared to other activities.

4.3.4 Family and Friends

"Family and friends" means all those people who are related to culture and in contact in to day to day activities, and with whom we share feelings and opinions through language. In the Sherpa-speaking community living in Kathmandu Valley, a different pattern of language use can be observed.

Table 4.7 demonstrates the use of various languages among Sherpa mother-tongue speakers while communicating with family members and friends. It shows that Sherpa is used with relatives within the family – father, mother, brother/ sister and spouse. Nepali is used among friends and neighbors outside. Figure 4.4 shows the same patterns of language use in Sherpa.

In Fig. 4.4, we see that mother tongue is used and is effective among relatives and friends inside family. When communicating outside with friends, relatives and neighbors, the use of Nepali is increasing and the use of Sherpa is decreasing.

Table 4.7 Domains of language use with family and friends

Persons		Languages				
		Sherpa	More Sherpa less Nepali	More Nepali less Sherpa	Nepali	Nepali and English
1.	Father	84.44%	4.44%	8.88%	4.44%	–
2.	Mother	84.44%	4.44%	8.88%	4.44%	–
3.	Brother/Sister	71.11%	8.88%	13.33%	6.66%	–
4.	Spouse	55.55%	6.66%	4.44%	6.66%	–
5.	Friends at home	33.33%	24.44%	26.66%	13.33%	2.22%
6.	Friends outside	4.44%	37.77%	4.44%	40.00%	13.33%
7.	Neighbor at home	11.11%	24.44%	11.11%	53.33%	–
8.	Neighbors outside	6.66%	31.11%	2.22%	60.00%	–

Source: Gautam (2018, 2020)

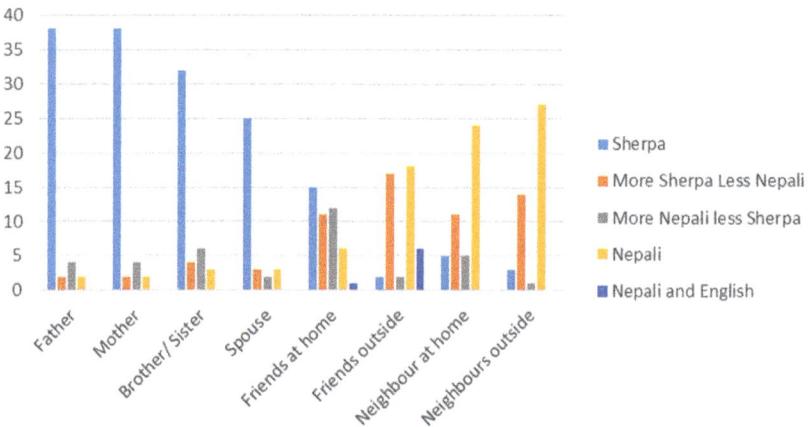

Fig. 4.4 Language use in family and friends. (Source: Gautam 2020)

4.3.5   *Media and Entertainments*

The Sherpa community also presents an interesting pattern of language use in the domains of media-related activities. Such activities include watching movies and serials on TV, watching news, listening to news and other programs on the radio, reading newspapers and reading horoscopes. Table 4.8 presents the domains of language use in media-related activities in the Sherpa community.

Figure 4.8 shows that the use of mother tongue (51.5%) is limited to listening music and that Nepali, English and Hindi languages are heavily used in activities like watching serials and news, listening to music and news as well as reading newspapers and horoscopes. This language use among the Sherpa community in the Kathmandu Valley is clearly presented in Fig. 4.5.

Figure 4.5 indicates that the Sherpa-speaking community living in Kathmandu Valley is shifting towards Nepali, English and Hindi in most media-related activities. The impact of media and entertainment on Sherpa is notable.

Table 4.8 Domains of language use in media-related activities

Activities		Language use				
		Sherpa	Nepali	English	Hindi	Others
1.	Watching movies/serials	2 (4.4%)	44 (97.8%)	18 (40.0%)	29 (64.45%)	1 (2.2%)
2.	Watching news	2 (4.4%)	45 (100.0%)	15 (33.3%)	7 (15.5%)	1 (2.2%)
3.	Listening to music	23 (51.1%)	36 (80.0%)	13 (28.9%)	15 (33.3%)	3 (6.6%)
4.	Listening to radio/news	2 (4.4%)	43 (95.5%)	14 (31.1%)	6 (12.3%)	1 (2.2%)
5.	Listening to interviews	3 (6.6%)	43 (95.5%)	11 (24.4%)	4 (8.9%)	–
6.	Reading newspapers	3 (6.6%)	37 (82.2%)	16 (35.5%)	1 (2.2%)	–
7.	Reading horoscopes	–	37 (82.2%)	8 (17.9%)	1 (2.2%)	–

Source: Gautam (2018, 2020)

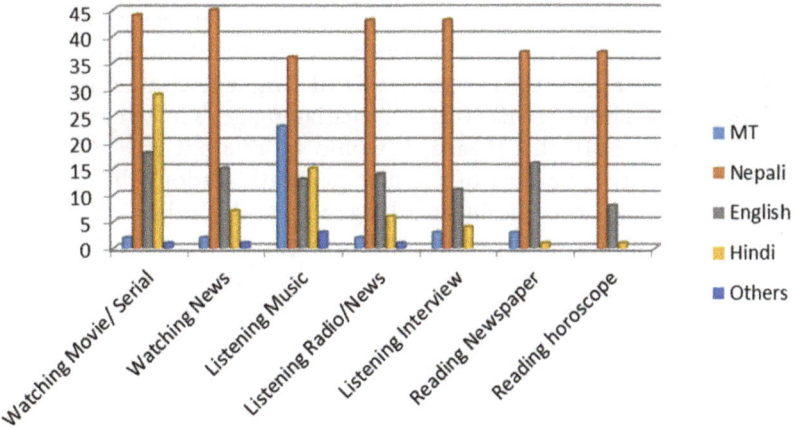

Fig. 4.5 Domains of language use in media-related activities. (Source: Gautam 2020)

4.4   Language Contact
and Intergenerational Shift

Language shift is the process by which a speech community in a contact situation (i.e. consisting of bi/multilingual speakers) gradually stops using one of its two languages in favor of the other. The causal factors of language shift are generally considered to be social. This study has been focused on speakers' attitudes (both explicit and unstated) towards language and domains of language use in the community. In addition, research has focused on the effects of language shift in Nepalese context.

Language shift, sometimes referred to as language transfer or language replacement or assimilation, is the process whereby a speech community of a language shifts to speak another language, usually over an extended period of time. The language shift may have different effects on a language community. There may be cultural shift along with language shift, and some different languages can emerge. Language shift is one of the consequences of globalization. Nepal's labor migration and market forces have their effect on language shift: Nepalese laborers working in foreign countries become acquainted with the languages used in those countries; as a result, there is language shift. There might also be communication problems between speakers of the same original language if they reside in different places and so are heavily influenced by different languages.

One significant concern in the study of language contact is related to how people choose to use one or other language/s from one generation to the next. In this regard, it would be relevant to see whether (and how far) the speakers of the new generation adopt their mother tongue or use another/additional language/s. Regarding the pattern of intergenerational shift of this kind, though all the domains of language use are not analyzed here, the domain of personal activities will be considered for a brief analysis.

Some indications of language shift can be noted in a couple of personal activities. For instance, the use of Sherpa mother tongue was not found in the age group of 15–25 years in the activity of telling stories to children or singing inside and outside, though older generation speakers are found to use Sherpa for the same activities.

More interesting is the case of language use is the activity of counting applicable in Sherpa. Absence of the use of Sherpa is noticeable in the age group 15–25, though it is present in older generations. However, younger generation Sherpas (15–25 years) were found using the mother tongue in all the personal activities covered by this study. Sherpa speakers living in Kathmandu use their mother tongue in the domains of cultural, religious and some of the formal situations as well. However, data indicates that the younger generation of mother tongue speakers is being gradually motivated to other "dominant" languages under the influence of globalization, education, migration, business and communication and technologies and the media.

In Kathmandu Valley, language is intimately linked to the sociocultural and political transformations that we have briefly outlined above. As we know, language shifts because of changing social realities. Multilingualism in vernaculars, lingua francas, and colonial and national languages that characterizes many multilingual communities is a clear product of contact. What happens to linguistic structures, practices and values mirrors, reinforces and sometimes changes presuppositions about social relations, and social relations themselves (Silverstein 1979: 223).

4.5   LANGUAGE ATTITUDE IN THE SHERPA COMMUNITY

Attitude can be defined as subjective evaluations of both language varieties and their speakers, whether the attitudes are held by individuals or by groups (Scotton 2005). This study of language attitude can help researchers understand two important relations: the relation between particular linguistic forms and social power, and the relation between language and literacy. Although the apparent softening of attitude towards indigenous languages, for instance Sherpa, among the population as a whole might seem a positive development in terms of support for language-maintenance measures, a negative attitude towards indigenous and minority languages and dialects has been included and internalized over centuries. This has been correctly pointed by Scotton (2005) as personal and group beliefs, mindsets and psychological or cognitive orientations affecting the decision that speakers and even nation states make about becoming or remaining bilingual. A condition for a language to spread is that there is a geographical opportunity for one language to spread into the domains of another language or languages (p. 213). The Sherpa of Kathmandu Valley have been migrating from different districts in the belief that Kathmandu and the city centers are better than their birthplaces in terms of employment, education, development and civilization.

A set of questions were administered to the Sherpa informants in order to examine attitudes towards different languages. The question, *"If there are two people coming to work at your place having same skills and expe-riences, one speaks Sherpa and another speaks Nepali, whom would you choose?*" was used to understand their attitude. In response to this, around two-thirds of the informants replied that they would choose the one with the mother tongue whereas slightly more than one-third of the informants had no preference. Figure 4.6 presents the different attitudes of common Sherpa people toward Nepali and Sherpa.

During the interview I asked people the reasons for their preference. The people who chose Sherpa said that it was very easy for them to com-municate and handle a new colleague because of cultural and ethnic simi-larity. They said that language brings people close to each other. On the other hand, the people who responded either attributed their choice to understanding of the language they know, that is Nepali or Sherpa. This creates various difficulties in bargaining and working conditions outside the community. They reacted that if the worker knows Sherpa, it is easy to share food and other cultural activities.

Figure 4.7 below presents the responses to the question "How often do you speak Nepali?

Figure 4.7 shows the highest frequency of Nepali language among the migrated Sherpa community living in Kathmandu Valley. Only 7% of the respondents replied that they use their mother tongue sometimes.

Similarly, I asked people about their reasons for using Nepali, the offi-cial and contact language of Nepal, and English, the lingua franca of the world. They responded differently. The r responses are illustrated in the (Fig. 4.8).

Fig. 4.6 Attitude toward Sherpa and Nepali. (Source: Gautam 2017)

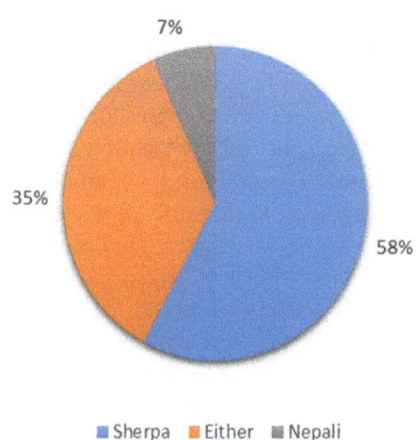

■ Sherpa ■ Either ■ Nepali

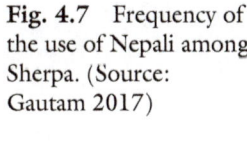

Fig. 4.7 Frequency of the use of Nepali among Sherpa. (Source: Gautam 2017)

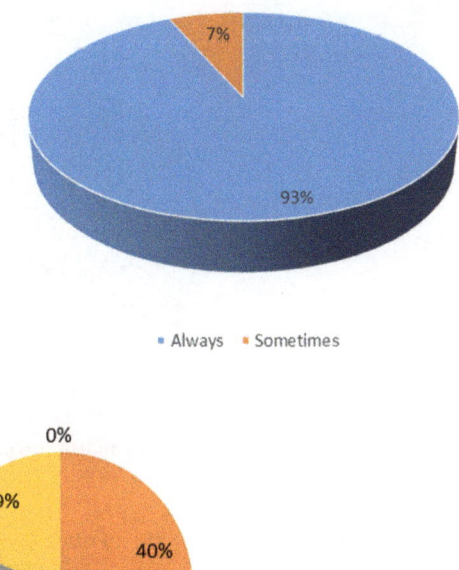

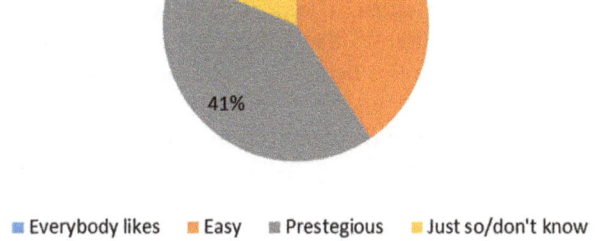

Fig. 4.8 Why do you like to use Nepali? (Source: Gautam 2017)

These responses show that they chose Nepali as it is extensively used in most of their everyday domains and activities. Endangered and minority languages are not spoken in isolation. Language shift is a response to a situation which involves contact with at least one another community in an unequal power relationship.

Figure 4.9 presents the responses to the question "Why do you like to use English?"

These responses about English suggest that language attitudes and ideologies are, of course, impossible to observe directly, so they have to be inferred using various techniques. Market research and opinion surveys

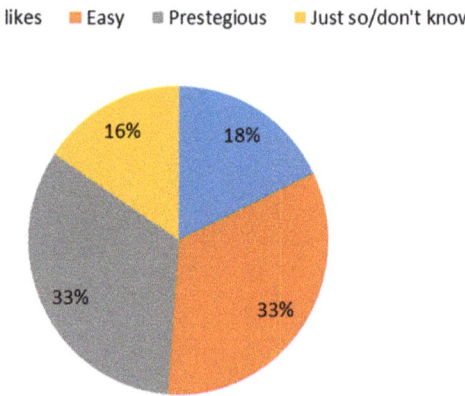

■ Everybody likes   ■ Easy   ■ Prestegious   ■ Just so/don't know

Fig. 4.9 Reasons for the use of English. (Source: Gautam 2017)

assume that attitudes can be deduced through direct questions, using standardized questionnaires; this is similar to the expression of Labov that the aim of linguistic research in the community must be to find out how people talk when they are not being systematically observed—yet we can only obtain such data by systematic observation (Labov 1972: 47).

A 19-year-old Sherpa girl (interviewed in February 2017) studying in school instantly responded

> *Sherpa bhasa ghrarma bolinchha tara yasko ke bahira phera ke kam chha ra*
> [Sherpa language is used only inside home but it does not have any value outside].

Saying this, she is emphasizing the value of Nepali language in Nepal and the importance of English language in international market.

Negative attitudes towards minority languages are common around the world. A commonsense assumption can be made that descendants of immigrants are less likely to speak the indigenous language. Sherpa living in Kathmandu city have been concerned and connected with various professions and academia that reflects their attitude towards languages in multilingual setting. On both at societal and an interpersonal level, the language that a person is able to speak is an index of that person's position society. A person's linguistic repertoire is source of symbolic power. Sociolinguistics often wants to understand what people think about the language they use or that other people use. People's beliefs and feelings are related to their linguistic behavior; and feelings about language forms impact people who use those forms; their beliefs and feelings are also interesting and have practical implications, for example in language policy and planning (Giles and Billings 2004: 46).

Multilingual institutions, such as workplaces, are prime sites for exploring multilingual language use and for examining the processes of second language socialization (Clyne and Ball 1990). The multilingual workplace is increasingly the norm in our ever-more globalized economy. Nepal is a developing country in south Asia where we can see the impact of globalization in education, tourism and business and the shifting lifestyle of the urban population. However, it will remain a site of struggle, with the relationship between dominant and minority language use acted out across issues of identity, rights and opportunities. Nepali is the official as well as contact language for all Sherpa people in Kathmandu. Contact Nepali among Sherpa speakers seems to be a connection of ideas and the feelings among the different ethnic groups who do not speak and understand each other's mother tongue.

4.6   Causes and Impact of Language Contact

This section deals with some major trends of language shift in Nepal, focusing on diverse domains of activities. Specifically, it examines the causes and impacts of such shifts in languages spoken by Sherpa people in Kathmandu Valley. The analysis of FGDs, individual interviews and field observations reveals the following causes and impacts.

4.6.1   Causes of Language Contact

4.6.1.1 Media, Migration and Marriage (M3)

The analysis of the research data demonstrates that there are many factors that promote language contact. Media, migration and marriage (M3) are found to play a vital role in contact and shift. Growing use of different media, whether electronic or print, exposes mother tongue speakers to regional and global languages. As is observed in Nepal's linguistic landscape, the influence of Nepali-, English- and Hindi-medium channels is strong. Such influence can be observed in people's growing consumption of Nepali channels, especially for news, entertainment and information about the diverse social, cultural and political aspects of the state; Hindi channels especially for entertainment; and English channels in order to get entertainment, sports and international/ global context. These days the fast-growing use of social sites in internet like Facebook, Twitter, Google, Skype and Viber has made the use of different languages easy and familiar.

Migration has become a prominent phenomenon in the population dynamics of Nepal. Emigration has been exceeding entry, which is thought to have had a considerable adverse effect on fertility. Migration has become another vigorous cause of language contact and shift in Kathmandu Valley. Kathmandu city had almost 42% internal migrants from both rural and urban areas of other districts (44% with foreign-born) in 2001. Dealing with the migration rate, the number of emigrants (out movers) per thousand population stands at 10.77, whereas the immigration rate is estimated to be 0.46 (CBS 2011). Migration and language intermingle in a complex, yet superficial way. Primarily, migration leads to language or dialect contact, and is certainly the main cause of such contact. Although the fact that migration differs greatly in time, distance and motivation, it has been possible to show that, given a particular collection of migration types and language varieties in contact, it is possible to make generalizations, and even realistic expectations, about the sociolinguistic outcomes of migration.

Nepal is currently experiencing the greatest internal as well as external migration rates in its history (CBS 2011). Internal migration is undertaken from rural villages to urban (cities) and semi-urban areas owing to the attractions of education, health and other modern facilities. External migration from Nepal to the Middle East, to Asian countries including India, Malaysia and South Korea, and to European and American countries, is largely undertaken for improving personal income, getting higher education, or for some other business purposes. Both are key factors that promote language shifts. As this analysis points out, internal migration has led to language shift from the local languages to Nepali, English and Hindi languages.

Language shift that depends on external migration can be observed in personal narratives. For example, a Sherpa girl (34 yrs.) said she learnt French and English languages in order to find her future career in France. She said,

My relatives especially those in France use English and French, I also communicate with them in these languages. Since I am planning to go to France for my

future, I am learning French and using it with my relatives in France.
(Interview, Angdiki, April 2017)

A similar situation was observed in the narratives of Pasang (42 yrs.), a Sherpa-speaking man who had been living in Thailand for the last six years. He said,

> *We don't find good jobs here, we have to leave for other countries for business, so I think we have to learn the languages, so we could adjust there.* (Interview, March 2017)

Angdiki and Pasang's narratives are just two examples among many from the respondents involved in this study. These stories, in one way or another, suggest how language shift, especially from local languages to regional or global languages, is strengthened by migration.

Marriage is another cause of migration that often promotes language shift. Marriage between individuals of interlingual background is instructive in understanding how it promotes language shift. It is helpful to reference the story of Phurba, a 33-year-old Sherpa-speaking woman here. She was running a hotel with her parents in Khumjung while studying at school. Later, a foreigner sponsored her and she came to Kathmandu. Two years ago, she got married to him (Peter) and now she is planning to go to New Zealand with him (Interview July 2017). For this she is learning English language for writing and speaking. Phurba says that her future is bright in New Zealand and she is also planning to take her parents with her. This story shows that not only intercaste marriage but marriages with foreigners can motivate people towards language shift. Neoliberal ideology is working in language contact and shift among the young Sherpa in Kathmandu.

4.6.1.2 Education

Education is one of the most effective causes of language shift, usually acting very quickly. The state's ideology to expose the young citizens to more dominant national, regional and international languages promotes language shift. This analysis often indicates that the Sherpa explored in this study is primarily used in its local contexts. The language has not been (well) accepted in formal schooling and academic institutions. Some efforts to educate young children in their mother tongue have been abandoned due to the lack of public interest, concrete policies on mother tongue education and parental desire to expose their children to more dominant languages such as Nepali and English. Since English-prioritized schooling access for children is often perceived as the symbol of better future, better social status and economic soundness of the household (Devkota 2018: 111), parents are more motivated to make their children learn English and Nepali languages instead of their mother tongue.

Lakpa, a student from Khumjung studying Hotel Management in Kathmandu says,

We are Sherpa and our main purpose to study in Kathmandu is to go to foreign country and to learn and earn money. Why to learn and speak Sherpa when there is no value? (Interview August 2017)

Lakpa's comment indicates how people of diverse local mother tongues shift to other dominant languages because of the limited opportunities they have had when using and exposing themselves with their mother tongue locally and globally.

In FGDs that took place in three major areas of Kathmandu Valley, the participants often explained how their children have been comprehensively exposed to Nepali and English in place of their mother tongues. Karma (47) is a trekking guide and seasonal migrant of Kathmandu city. He speaks broken English and good Nepali. His wife runs a small liquor shop in Kapan but he sends his two children to a boarding school in order to improve their English. His personal narrative indicates that schooling/education is crucial in promoting and shaping language shift. Schools' emphasis on dominant state or global languages ultimately isolates young people from their mother tongue.

4.6.1.3 Travel and Tourism

Nepal is not only linguistically and culturally varied, but also ecologically and geographically different. Due to its diversity in geography as well as its exceptional climate, Nepal has a wide variety of plant and animal species and is famous for its vegetation and wildlife, beautiful rivers and lakes. Nepal is the land of world's highest peak, *Sagarmatha* (Mt. Everest), Lumbini, the birth place of Buddha, Janakpur, the birthplace of Janaki and the Pashupatinath temple which visitors from across the world visit for different purposes. Every year, thousands of people visit Nepal, for many reasons. Some of them are on holiday, while some of them want to study the languages and cultures of the people and the country's natural resources. For all of these visitors, whatever their national language, English plays a significant role as a medium of communication, from booking tickets and hotels to arranging travel and trekking during their stay in Nepal.

Most of the Sherpa associated with the travel and tourism industry, such as hotel, restaurant and trekking entrepreneurs, need knowledge of English. Not everyone involved in this business is highly educated; some are illiterate and run small lodges and restaurants. They spontaneously develop competency in foreign languages like English, Hindi and Chinese through direct contact with foreigners so that most Sherpa people involved in this field understand and speak these languages. Thus, travel and tourism is an important factor in language contact and shift from local to foreign languages.

4.6.1.4 Market Forces and Economic Benefits

Market forces are intimately connected to the economic benefits of individuals' acquisition of dominant languages. This study exhibits a number of examples from diverse study sites where people are shifting their language for business and economic reasons.

Mobility has to be taken into consideration when discussing the linguistic situation in Nepal. People migrate from one place to another for economic reasons. Rural Nepalese relocate to such cities as Kathmandu and assume de-ethnicized urban identities. They feel proud of being permanent residents of a big city. Speaking Nepali has become associated with high-income groups, not ethnic identity (Eagle 2000: 21).

Current market forces are seen to be imperative in language shift in different ways. The growing trend of external migration of Nepali citizens in the international labor market encourages them to learn a particular language(s) that benefits them in a new social context, no matter that it is extensively for instrumental purposes in the beginning; language shift ultimately ensues. A Sherpa-speaking man (48) in Kathmandu observed,

> *What I think is the current globalization trend has some more effect on the languages we use, for example, I speak Sherpa, Nepali and English and Hindi to get better jobs in the labor market outside the country.* (Interview, February 2017)

Similarly, another Sherpa-speaking man (38) from Dolakha commented,

Where are our languages, I mean Sherpa, Tharu, Bhojpuri?... in media we listen to Nepali and English, even Hindi rather than our local languages, we read English, Nepali, Hindi ... in the advertisements and manuals of materials we buy at home ... we have to go to other countries for work or study, so what happens if we don't learn these languages?

The participants' comments clearly indicate why people are motivated to acquire languages such as Nepali in the national context, and English or other dominant languages under the influence of market forces and economic benefits.

4.6.1.5 Political-Ideological Intervention

Political-ideological intervention of the state is another powerful cause promoting language shift through contact. The 1959 and 1962 Constitutions of Nepal confer the status of the national language to Nepali. The term "Nepali", as it used for language, was made popular by missionaries and British scholars. The feeling of Nepali linguistic nationalism that grew in India was able to replace the terms like *Khas Kura, Parbatiya* or *Gorkhali* in the later days, which influenced the authorities in Nepal and the title *Gorkha Bhasa Prakasini Samiti* was changed to Nepali (Bandhu 1989). The Nepali version of *Ramayana* by Bhanubhakta Acharya(1814–1869) was brought to light through its publication by another Nepali literary figure, Moti Ram Bhatta (1866–1896). With Moti Ram Bhatta, thus the Nepali language entered into the age of printing. The domain of Nepali language was widely extended into various genres of literature (Bandhu 1989). With the establishment of the *Gorkha Bhasa Prakasini Samiti* (Gorkha language publishing house) in 1913 some efforts were made to make Nepali a stable language. A secular and modern Nepali literature began to flourish with the publication of the literary monthly *Sarada*[2] in 1934. Thus, although Nepali language had been the court language for two hundred years, its popular flowering is a recent phenomenon.

During the past century, Nepali has taken great strides to raise itself to the status of the national language. Although studies on the comprehension and the use of Nepali by non-Nepali speakers are few and far between, sheer expediency seems to have driven more and more non-Nepali speakers to use and understand it in their day-to-day transactions, interethnic communications and, above all, in their dealings with the channels of the local and national administration. Since the very instigation of modern

Nepal, the Nepali language has been highlighted as the language of unity, the language of social harmony and national integration. In addition, Nepali has been intensively employed in schooling/ education, media and formal communication in the state. Such intervention has promoted the Nepali language throughout the nation.

Due to the lack of a concrete plan by the Nepalese government regarding the development of ethnic languages, the English language, along with Nepali, has become predominant in school curricula, both in rural and urban parts of Nepal. The learning of English provides Nepalese with opportunities to obtain jobs in various national and international governmental organizations and in the media. Therefore, a large section of the Nepalese people is attracted to the English language more than other local languages.

As has been explored in the interviews and FGDs, the growing shift to Nepali and English language is because of their extensive use and applicability in formal situations, media, education and other formal fields. Narratives of respondents from diverse socioeconomic backgrounds demonstrate that their shifts to Nepali and English language are mostly related to fulfilling pragmatic purposes.

4.6.2   Impacts of Language Shift

4.6.2.1   Ideological/Attitudinal Impact

Language has a crucial role in the ideological process. It is the linking element between individuals' knowledge of the world and their social practices, since it mediates individual thought and behavior. This study demonstrates how Sherpa language reflects ideology and can thus be used not only as a means of communication, but also as an instrument of power and control. The linguistic texture of urban areas in the world can be described as a combination of regional majority languages, a wide range of migrant languages, foreign languages which are learnt by considerable parts of school population, and English as the actual lingua franca in many domains of life (Blommaert 2010). As the data demonstrate, the use of mother tongues is concentrated in households and the immediate surrounding communities in religious and cultural activities. Nonetheless, there exists a significant generation gap in the language used in such activities. The younger generations of this language community use Nepali and English more than they use the mother tongue, that is Sherpa, in these domains. People often relate their mother tongues to their ethnic identity and highlight its importance for maintaining communal solidarity (CS). However, they relate their shift to Nepali and English to more pragmatic/instrumental values, including intercultural contacts. Sherpa who attend boarding schools are typically not exploring new ways to be Sherpa in the city. Rather, they are being enculturated into Nepali urban life, not least by speaking Nepali exclusively. Kroskrity (2000) emphasizes the fact that distinct ethnic identities of minority groups, for example, must be created from linguistic symbols and/or communicative practices that differ in resources available for the construction of other ethnic identities or more generally, available national identities (p. 112). This raises an interesting point: Sherpa that live in Nepal are more patriotic than other ethnic communities. They are clearly proud of this distinction. However, it does not typically undermine their identity as a Sherpa. For instance, if one were to ask Ngima (a Sherpa who was born and raised in the Khumbu and who feels very closely tied to Sherpa culture and the language) where he was from, he would likely say "Nepal," yet he would also qualify that he is a Sherpa. Interestingly enough, Rinzi, who speaks very little Sherpa and who has been altogether distanced from Sherpa culture for his entire life, responded in the same way. Being Sherpa, then, is equally important as being Nepali. For Sherpa like Ngima, the Sherpa language is the key to this distinction. Ngawang Sherpa explains it well:

> *The Sherpa language is very important to represent the true identity. There is a linkage between tradition, culture, religion, norms and other values and the language. If we forget our language, we lose our identity in the long run.* (Ngawang, 2017, March)

These observations indicate that many ethnic groups, whether outside of their indigenous homeland or not, feel pressures from the flow of people and the larger, more widely spoken languages that they speak to assimilate. Such worries are made clear in attempts at understanding language loss, strategic code switching, and language revitalization efforts.

4.6.2.2 Motivational Impact
During the interviews we asked participants to give their reasons for choosing languages. The people who chose Sherpa said that it is very easy for them to communicate and handle because of cultural and ethnic similarity. They said that language makes people to be close each other while sharing food and language.

Hamro vasa ramro chha tara koi bujhdaina ani yo chhorachhoriharu pani bolna mandaina sarkar pani kunai niti lyauduina k garnu hajur [Our language is very beautiful but nobody understands. Our children do not speak and the government does not have any policy to preserve it.]. (A Sherpa man, 65)

This simple but very important reaction of a Sherpa man throws light on the present language policy and the hidden motivation towards Sherpa language. A multiplicity of language ideologies can often be found within a community, reflecting divergent perspectives associated with social groups that hold differing interests and positions within a society (Makihara 2007: 62)

As discussed earlier, people are more motivated to learn the languages of wider communication (in terms of population and space) instead of the home language while communicating outside, as well as for formal purposes, different occasions and circumstances. While using the mother tongue at home and with family, Sherpa people have the feeling that their language is for regulating their own cultural and religious activities. Despite this, they raise questions over the practical relevance of their mother tongue in formal, official and administrative situations as well. In many circumstances, people did not believe in the possibility of making use of their mother tongue for the purposes of educational, administrative and similar formal work. In the case of the Sherpa language, respondents very often identified Nepali as the language for formal activities and contact with people of other mother tongues. As a result of the continuing shift from Sherpa to Nepali, there is increasing influence and motivation of Nepali mother tongue-speaking people in urban areas like Kathmandu. As the use of local language diminishes in formal situations and activities, people tend to think that Nepali and English occupy a higher position than their local mother tongue. This sort of feeling can be found even though they use their local mother tongue at home and within limited social surroundings.

4.7   Summary

Sherpa is widely used in cultural and religious activities. Nepali is dominantly used in social, official, ceremonial and media-related activities. English and Hindi languages are used in media, ceremonial and official activities. The influence of English is increasing and is much higher than

Hindi, which indicates that Sherpa are motivated towards globalization and Western traditions. Sherpa have been directly involved in tourism and trekking, and the contact with many foreigners motivates them towards English rather than other languages. Migrated Sherpa living in the capital city have been directly and indirectly motivated by globalization and international trade and communication. Moreover, they have been involved in various social, cultural and ceremonial activities within the new mixed society which motivates them to shift to new target languages from the ancestral source language. Existing political, social and economic factors contribute to language contact and shift. Nepali, the dominant language in the capital city, the lingua franca of the country, and English, the international language for various purposes, are becoming more valuable and influential in the Sherpa community, which is an indication of language shift and endangerment.

NOTES

1. Percentages exceeding 100 indicate multiple entries in the data.
2. The first literary magazine in Nepali.

BIBLIOGRAPHY

Bandhu, C. M. (1989). The role of national language in establishing the national unity. *Kailash, 15,* 121–134.

Blommaert, J. (2010). *The sociolinguistics of globalization.* Cambridge and New York: Cambridge University Press.

Central Bureau of Statistics. (2011). *Population of Nepal.* Kathmandu: National Planning Commission.

Clyne, M., & Ball, M. (1990). English as a lingua franca, especially in industry. *Australian Review of Applied Linguistics,* Series S, No. 7, 1–15.

Devkota, K. R. (2018). Navigating exclusionary-inclusion: Experience of Dalit school children in rural Nepal. *Globe: Journal of Language, Culture and Communication, 6,* 106–120. Alborg: Alborg University Press.

Eagle, S. (2000). The language situation in Nepal. In R. B. Baldauf & R. B. Kaplan (Eds.), *Language Planning in Nepal, Taiwan and Sweden* (pp. 170–225). Sydney: Multilingual Matters Ltd.

Gautam, B. L. (2012). Contact Nepali in Kathmandu valley: Convergence between TB & IA languages. *Nepalese Linguistics, 27,* 38–42.

Gautam, B. L. (2017). Language use and attitude among the Sherpa speaking community in Kathmandu valley. *Gipan, 3*(2), 26–37. Kathmandu, Central Department of linguistics, TU.

Gautam, B. L. (2018). Language shift in Newar: A case study in the Kathmandu valley. *Nepalese Linguistics, 33*(1), 33–42.

Gautam, B. L. (2020). *Language contact in Kathmandu.* An unpublished PhD dissertation, Tribhuvan University, Kathmandu.

Giles, H., & Billings, A. (2004). Assessing language attitudes: Speaker evaluation studies. In A. Davies & C. Elder (Eds.), *The handbook of applied linguistics* (pp. 187–205). Oxford, UK: Blackwell Publishing.

Kroskrity, P. V. (2000). Regimenting languages: Language ideological perspectives. In P. V. Kroskrity (Ed.), *Regimes of language: Ideologies, polities, and identities.* Santa Fe, NM: School of American Research Press.

Labov, W. (1972). *Sociolinguistic pattern.* Philadelphia: University of Pennsylvania Press.

Makihara, M. (2007). Linguistic purism in Rapa Nui political discourse. In M. Makihara & B. B. Shiefflin (Eds.), *Consequences of contact: Language ideologies and socio-cultural transformations in Pacific societies.* London: Oxford University Press.

Scotton, C.-M. (2005). *Multiple voices: An introduction to bilingualism.* Wiley-Blackwell.

Silverstein, M. (1979). Language structure and linguistic ideology. In P. R. Clyne, W. F. Hanks, & C. L. Hofbauer (Eds.), *The elements: A para session on linguistic units and levels* (pp. 193–247). Chicago: Chicago Linguistic Society.

CHAPTER 5

Language Contact in Newar

5.1 Introduction

This chapter presents an outline of the various aspects of language contact in Newar. It consists of five sections: Sect. 5.2 introduces the Newar people and language and its profile in Kathmandu Valley; Sect. 5.3 examines different patterns of language use in Newar; Sect. 5.4 deals with language contact and intergenerational shift; Sect. 5.5 is related to the causes and impacts of language contact in Newar; Sect. 5.6 summarizes the main findings of the chapter.

5.2 Newar People and Language

This section offers a brief introduction to the Newar people and language.

5.2.1 The Newar People

The Newar are the indigenous inhabitants of Kathmandu Valley, namely Kathmandu (Newar name *Ye*), Lalitpur (*Yela*) and Bhaktapur (*Khopa*) and other urban areas across the country. The civilization and cultures of Kathmandu Valley are identified with the Newar civilization and culture. Nepali (1965) has observed that the Newars are people with a high degree of material culture and a distinctive social organization. The origin of the Newars, however, still remains uncertain and the proto identity of the Newar people continues to be disputed among various schools of thought.

© The Author(s), under exclusive license to Springer Nature
Switzerland AG 2021
B. L. Gautam, *Language Contact in Nepal*,
https://doi.org/10.1007/978-3-030-68810-3_5

Newar society is divided into two broad religious groups, Buddhists and the Hindus. Both of these groups are subject to further classifications based on the hierarchy of caste relations and social/ professional status. The overview of this complex caste structure is summarized in Table 5.1,

Table 5.1   The Newar caste hierarchy and the traditional professions

SN	Names of Castes/ Communities	Traditional professions
Buddhist Newars		
1.	*Bajracharya*	Tantric priests (*Gubhaaju/ Guru-ju*)
2.	*Shakya*	Gold/ silversmiths (*Barhe/ Bade*)
3.	*Tuladhar*	Traders/ Merchants
4.	*Kansakar*	Bronze/ alloy metal craftsmen (*Kasaa:*)
5.	*Tamrakar*	Coppersmiths (Tabah)
6.	Baniya	Dealers in spices, herbal drugs
7.	*Sthapit*	Builders & Carpenters (*SyiKa:mi*)
8.	*Sikhrakar*	Builders, Roof-layers (*Aawaa*)
9.	*Sindurakar*	Wood carvers & Image makers
10.	*Shilakar*	Stonemasons & sculptors (*Lohā Ka:mi*)
11.	*Shilalik (Kathmandu)*	Pastrymakers, confectioners (*Madhi-kā:mi*)
12.	*Rajkarnikar (Lalitpur)*	Pastrymakers, confectioners (*Halwaai*)
13.	*Manandhar*	Oil-pressers (*Saaymi*)
14.	*Prajapati*	Potters (*Kumaah*)
15.	*Kisan*	Farmers (*Jyaapu*)
Hindu Newars		
1.	*Joshi*	Astrologers (*Jotish*)
2.	*Rajopadhyaya*	Priests of Hindu Newars (*Dya: Baramhu*)
3.	*Vaidya*	Ayurvedic physicians
4.	*Shrestha*	Moneylenders (*Shesya:*)
5.	*Rajbhandari*	Royal palace treasurer/ storekeeper
6.	*Tandukar*	Grain merchants
7.	*Malakar*	Gardeners/ florists(*Gathu*)
8.	*Ranjitkar*	Cloth dryers & design printers(*Chipaa*)
9.	*Chitrakar*	Artists/ painters (*Pu:*)
10.	*Nakarmi*	Blacksmiths (*Kau*)
11.	*Suchikar*	Tailors/ traditional band players
12.	*Kasaai/Khadki*	Butchers (*Naay*)
13.	*Napit*	Barbers (*Naau*)
14.	*Dhobi*	Washermen (*Dhobya*)
15.	*Sarki*	Cobblers/ leather shoe makers
16.	*Dabaai*	Players of wind instruments
17.	*Dalli*	Forest dwellers/ foragers
18.	*Majhi*	Fishermen(*Podyaa*)
19.	*Chyami*	Sweepers/ garbage collectors(*Chyamaa kalah*)

Source: *The sociolinguistic survey of the Newar language* (2011)

which is arranged in an approximate hierarchical order in relation to traditional professions. The Newar names, where applicable, are given in brackets, presenting a brief classification of different Newar castes/ communities and their professions.

Other Hindu Newars include *Amatya, Malla, Pradhan, Mathema, Maskey, Gurubacharya, Karmacharya, Kasaju/ Kayastha* and *Kapali*. The 2001 Census reported a total of 1,245,232 (5.4%) ethnic Newars, and 825,458 (3.03%) mother-tongue speakers which indicated a decline of 33.7% in active speakers. Census 2011 reported that there were 1,321,933 ethnic Newars and 846,557 (3.2%) mother tongue speakers. Some people view this trend as alarming, but the Newars continue to use their language extensively in many domains of sociocultural contexts, trade and commerce, education, literature and mass media. Table 5.2 shows the Newar population in different censuses.

Although Newar populations increased between the 1952/1954 and 2011 censuses, by 2011 the Newar group was no longer the biggest group in Kathmandu district, simply because a large number of Hill Brahman populations and other groups migrated into Kathmandu Valley because of the Maoist insurgency of 1996 to 2006 for reasons of security and employment. In addition, every year many people migrate into Kathmandu Valley for the purposes of jobs, education, business, etc. and eventually settle in Kathmandu district. Table 5.3 presents a short summary of Newar population in Kathmandu according to the censuses of 2001 and 2011.

Table 5.3 shows that the Newar population increased from 2001 to 2011 census but if we compare the total population of valley and nation, the percentage is not significantly changed.

Table 5.2 Newar mother tongue population in different censuses

SN	Census year	Total population	Percentage of national population
1	1952/1954	383,184	4.65%
2	1961	377,721	4.01%
3	1971	454,979	3.94%
4	1981	448,746	2.99%
5	1991	690,007	3.73%
6	2001	825,458	3.63%
7	2011	846,557	3.20%

Source: Census reports of Nepal

Table 5.3   Newar population in two censuses

SN	Districts	2001			2011		
		Total	Male	Female	Total	Male	Female
1	Kathmandu	295,439	146,279	149,160	383,136	190,297	192,839
2	Lalitpur	138,938	68,386	70,552	155,604	76,703	78,901
3	Bhakatapur	126,592	63,098	63,494	138,873	69,239	69,634
Grand Total		560,969	277,763	283,206	677,613	336,239	341,374

Source: CBS (2001a, 2011)

After the 1990 People's Movement that brought the Panchayat system to an end, the languages of Nepal enjoyed greater freedom. The 1991 constitution valued Nepal as a multiethnic and multilingual country. In 1997, Kathmandu Metropolitan City declared that its policy of officially recognizing Nepal Bhasa (the Newari language) would be revived. The rest of the city governments in the Kathmandu Valley announced that they too would recognize it. However, critics petitioned the Supreme Court to have the policy annulled, and as a result in 1999, the Supreme Court quashed the decision of the local bodies as being unconstitutional. However, various people and organizations have been working for the development of Newari language and culture. Newari has several newspapers, primary level to university level curricula, several schools, several FM stations (selected time for Newar programs), regular TV programs and news (on Image TV Channel), Nepal Bhasa Music Award (a part of Image Award) and several websites (including a Wikipedia in Nepal Bhasa). The impact and influence of these media and the heavy migration of the people in Kathmandu brought noticeable changes in language contact and shift.

5.2.2   The Newar Language

Newar or Newari (Nepal Bhasa[1]) is a Tibeto-Burman language spoken by the Newar people. Although Nepal Bhasa literally means Nepalese language, it is not the same as Nepali, the present official language of Nepal. The two languages belong to different language families (Tibeto-Burman and Indo-Aryan, respectively), but centuries of contact have resulted in a significant body of shared vocabulary. Both languages have official status in Kathmandu Metropolitan City. Newar was Nepal's administrative language from the fourteenth to the late eighteenth century (Malla 2015).

From the early twentieth century until the 1990 multiparty revolution, Newar suffered from political and official suppression. From 1952 to 1991, the percentage of Newar speakers in the Kathmandu Valley dropped from 75% to 44%, and today Newar culture and language are under threat. The language has been listed as being "definitely endangered" by the United Nations Educational and Scientific and Cultural Organization (UNESCO). The typological and genetic classification of Newar has been controversial for several reasons. A contributing factor has been the long periods of contact with Sanskrit, Prakrit and other Indic languages resulting in considerable lexical and grammatical borrowings, which in turn has tended to obscure its genetic relationships.

Linguists, including Kamal Prakash Malla, Tej Ratna Kansakar and others, connect the difficulty about the placement of Newar to the inability of scholars to connect it with the migration patterns of Tibeto-Burman speakers (personal communication). Since Newar separated from rest of the family very early in history, it is difficult or at least arbitrary to reconstruct the basic stratum that contributed to the present-day Newar language.

5.3   Domains of Language Use in Newar

This section mainly deals with the trends and patterns of language contact and shift, focusing on the diverse domains of language use and attitudes among the Newar speakers living in Kathmandu Valley. The trends and patterns of contact noticed in Newar languages are described under the following subsections which are based on informants' responses regarding the use of languages in various activities.

5.3.1   Informal Situations

Informal situations are those situations in which people do various activities informally without being conscious of or caring about the outer community. The informal situations in this speech community comprise two types of activities: behavioral and personal. They are briefly discussed below.

5.3.1.1 Behavioral Activities
Behavioral activities in this research mean those activities which indicate the different psychological behavior of informants. They include activities such as making friends, reading and writing, making telephone calls,

Table 5.4 Domains of language use in behavioral activities

Activities		Languages				
		Newar	Nepali	English	Hindi	Others
1.	Making friends	73.33%	93.33%	15.55%	6.66%	–
2.	Shopping	71.11%	97.77%	6.66%	35.55%	–
3.	Making telephone calls	80.00%	93.33%	22.22%	6.66%	–
4.	Talking with workers	60.00%	93.33%	22.22%	13.33%	–
5.	Talking with teachers/ professors	22.22%	93.33%	35.55%	–	–
6.	Talking with academics	28.88%	95.55%	26.66%	–	2.22%
7.	Getting a job	13.33%	77.77%	40.00%	–	–
8.	Reading and writing	35.55%	91.11%	46.66%	–	–
9.	Sitting exams	–	66.66%	42.22%	–	–

Source: Gautam (2020)

talking with different people, shopping and sitting exams. The domains of language use in different behavioral activities are presented in Table 5.4.

Table 5.4 shows that Nepali language is used heavily in almost all the domains in comparison to Newari, English and Hindi. The influence of English is much higher than that of Hindi because of education, globalization and tourism among the Newar-speaking community in Kathmandu Valley. Newar predominates in making friends, shopping, telephone calls and talking with workers rather than other activities. The use of English is very high for reading/ writing, sitting exams, getting jobs and talking with teachers and academics.

5.3.1.2 Personal Activities

Personal activities in this research means those activities which are connected to the personal and interpersonal activities of the informants. They include the activities such as joking, singing, praying, bargaining, abusing and telling stories. Similarly, Table 5.5 shows the different patterns of language use in personal activities. Newar, Nepali and English languages are used in most of the activities like joking, singing, praying, bargaining with higher frequency than Hindi and other languages. Here, the use of Hindi is very low as it is not necessary for use in informal personal activities. This pattern of language use in the Newar community in the Kathmandu Valley is presented in Fig. 5.1.

Table 5.5 Domains of language use in formal activities

Situations		Languages				
		Newar	Nepali	English	Hindi	Others
1.	Office/ Workplace	33.30%	8.44%	15.55%	4.44%	–
2.	Political/ Social gathering	44.44%	88.88%	2.22%	–	–
3.	Public activities/ Fun fair	51.11%	88.88%	4.44%	–	–
4.	Administration	6.66%	97.77%	8.88%	–	–
5.	Strangers	8.88%	97.77%	4.44%	2.22%	–

Source: Gautam (2020)

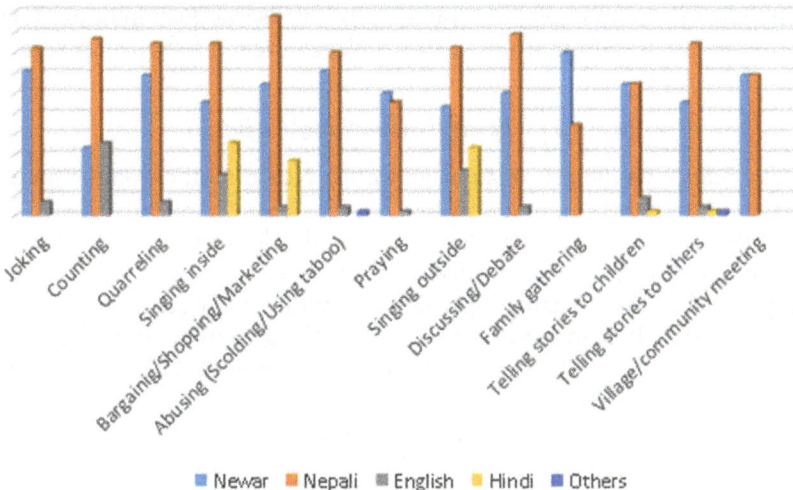

Fig. 5.1 Language use in personal activities. (Source: Gautam 2020)

Figure 5.1, shows that Newar language is dominant among the Newar mother tongue speakers in the activities of joking, quarrelling, verbal abusing, family gathering and village/ community meetings or gatherings. Nepali language is more dominant in the activities of singing inside and outside, counting, discussing and shopping/ marketing. The presence of Hindi is clearly noticeable in the activities of shopping and singing inside and outside. English is used in most of the activities except family gathering. The diagram also demonstrates that both Newar and Nepali languages are found in the activities of village/ community meeting, telling stories to children and telling stories to others.

From close observation of the information given above and interview transcripts (FGD/ individual) collected in the field, it is apparent that Nepali language is gradually becoming dominant among Newar mother tongue speakers. As a Newar man (56) commented,

> *We use Newar language at home and community since we are all Newars here; but when we go to our children's schools, or go to Shahar (Kathmandu city) for shopping, we use Nepali, so I know both languages and need both for different situations.* (Interview, February 2018)

Though a single example, the comment of this Newar man indicates how language use is shifting from Newar to Nepali even in personal activities.

5.3.2   Formal Situations/Activities

Table 5.5 shows the use of language among Newar mother tongue speakers in formal situations and activities.

Table 5.5 indicates that Nepali is highly dominant among Newar mother tongue speakers in formal situations. Nepali is also very influential in political and social gatherings, administration, public activities and funfair activities. It is interesting to see that Newar, rather than Nepali, is highly dominant in office and workplaces. As commented by many literate people of typical Newar communities in Kathmandu, the fundamental reason for people shifting from Newar to Nepali and other languages is that it is no longer taught in schools (whereas it was taught in schools previously). In some cases, English is found more to be more dominant than the Newar language. The presence of Nepali and English among Newar speakers in this manner implies the process of shifting from Newar to Nepali and English.

The dominance of Nepali among the Newar mother tongue speakers can be observed in the personal stories of the participants as well. As a Newar woman (65 years) comments,

> *Children these days speak either Nepali or English; they use Newar language only when we Newar-speaking parents and grandparents talk to them; they do not prefer to speak in Newar; they mix up Nepali and English words even if they speak Newar at all.* (Interview, February 2018)

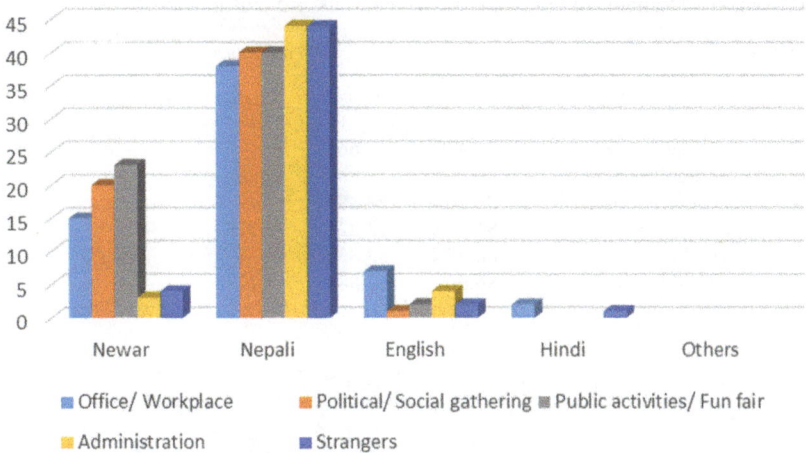

Fig. 5.2   Language use in formal situations. (Source: Gautam 2018, 2020)

The same interpretation is presented in Fig. 5.2.

Figure 5.2 indicates that Nepali language has a very dominant position in almost all formal activities and situations. The use of Newar in these situations is decreasing day by day. English language use is increasing in many formal situations because of privatization and global impact.

5.3.3   *Religious and Cultural Activities*

Newar speakers living in Kathmandu Valley use different languages in religious and cultural activities. Table 5.6 demonstrates the trend of language use among Newar mother tongue speakers in such activities.

Table 5.6 shows that the presence of Newar and Nepali languages can be seen in all the activities listed here under the domains of religious and cultural activities. However, use of Newar language is dominant in each and every case. English is very rare in cultural programs, the marriage ceremony and cultural festivals, and the use of Hindi is almost zero in the data. Figure 5.3 indicates Newar informants' language use in different religious and cultural activities.

Table 5.6   Domains of language use in religious and cultural activities

Activities		Languages				
		Newar	*Nepali*	*English*	*Hindi*	*Others*
1.	Religious Festivals	84.44%	26.66%	–	–	–
2.	Cultural Programs	80.00%	48.88%	2.22%	–	–
3.	Death Ceremonies	86.66%	28.88%	–	–	–
4.	Marriage Ceremonies	86.66%	42.22%	2.22%	–	–
5.	Birth Ceremonies	88.88%	33.33%	–	–	–
6.	Cultural Festivals	86.66%	48.88%	2.22%	–	–

Source: Gautam (2018, 2020)

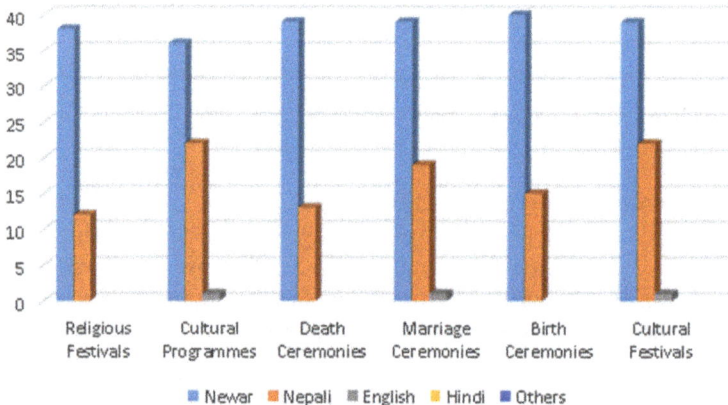

Fig. 5.3   Language use in religious and cultural activities. (Source: Gautam 2018, 2020)

Figure 5.3 indicates that Newar is heavily used in most religious and cultural activities. We can see the increasing influence of Nepali in cultural programs and different ceremonies. The impact of English can also be observed in cultural programs and marriage ceremonies.

5.3.4   Family and Friends

The Table 5.7 demonstrates language use of Newar mother tongue speakers while communicating with family members and friends.

In Table 5.7, we can see the presence of Nepali and Newar languages in all the cases. The Newar people may use both Nepali and Newar languages while talking with father, mother, brother, sister, spouse and friends at home but Newar is dominant. While communicating with friends outside the home, use of Nepali is more dominant; but Newar is more dominant when talking with neighbors outside the home. A number of Newar-speaking respondents used more Nepali than Newar with brother, sister, friends and neighbors outside the home. This is for ease of communication among the people. The same information is presented in Fig. 5.4 below.

Figure 5.4 indicates that Newar is widely used among family members, friends and relatives and neighbors inside the home, but Nepali and other languages are used among relatives and friends outside.

Table 5.7   Domains of language use in family and friends

Persons		Languages				
		Always Newar	More Newar less Nepali	More Nepali less Newar	Always Nepali	Nepali and English
1	Father	87%	8.88%	–	11.11%	–
2	Mother	84.44%	6.66%	–	8.88%	–
3	Brother/ Sister	77.77%	2.22%	4.44%	15.55%	–
4	Spouse	53.33%	2.22%	–	8.88%	–
5	Friends at home	51.11%	26.66%	2.22%	20.00%	–
6	Friends outside	15.55%	24.44%	15.55%	31.11%	13.33%
7	Neighbor at home	55.55%	13.33%	8.88%	22.22%	–
8	Neighbors outside	31.11%	26.66%	11.11%	31.11%	–

Source: Gautam (2018, 2020)

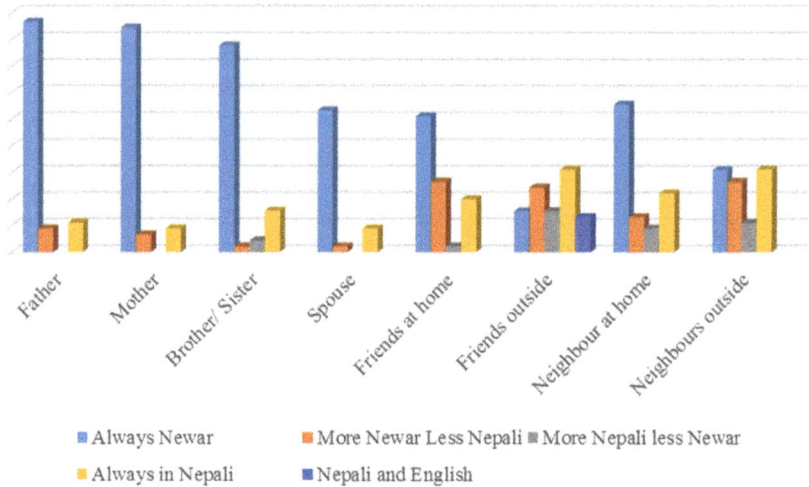

Fig. 5.4 Language use in family and friends. (Source: Gautam 2018)

5.3.5   *Media and Entertainments*

Table 5.8 presents the trend of language use among Newar mother tongue speakers in activities under the domain of media and entertainment.

Table 5.8 shows that Nepali language is dominant in media and entertainment activities compared to Newar. As the data indicate, many Newar mother tongue speakers use their native language in the activities of watching TV serials, TV news and listening to music; however, Nepali is dominant in these activities. In the activities of listening to news, listening and watching interviews, reading newspapers and reading horoscopes, Nepali has a wide dominance among Newari mother tongue speakers. Hindi language seems to occupy more space in the activity of watching TV serials and listening to music. English marks its presence in media and entertainment activities, notably watching TV serials and reading newspapers. However, these languages (Hindi and English) are not as widely used as Nepali is in media and entertainment activities. Figure 5.5 below shows the same pattern in different way.

Figure 5.5 indicates the impacts of language contact and shift among the Newar-speaking community living in Kathmandu Valley towards Nepali, English and Hindi. This shows that mother tongue is less popular in such activities.

Table 5.8 Domains of language use in media and entertainment

Activities	Languages				
	Newar	Nepali	English	Hindi	Others
1. Watching movie/ serial	35.55%	80.00%	33.33%	75.55%	20.00%
2. Watching news	22.22%	97.77%	17.77%	28.88%	–
3. Listening to music	57.77%	84.44%	37.77%	77.77%	–
4. Listening to radio/news	42.22%	97.77%	24.44%	11.11%	–
5. Listening to interviews	40.00%	97.77%	22.22%	22.22%	–
6. Reading newspaper	28.88%	82.22%	33.33%	4.44%	–
7. Reading horoscope	20.00%	93.33%	33.33%	2.22%	–

Source: Gautam (2018, 2020)

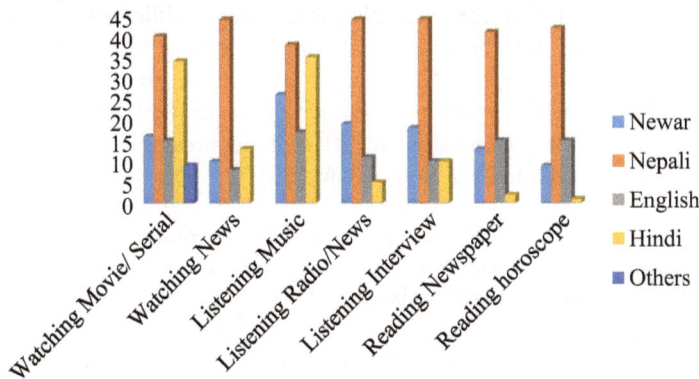

Fig. 5.5 Language use in media and entertainments. (Source: Gautam 2018)

5.4 Language Contact and Intergenerational Shift

Language contact leads to language shift from source language to target language. It is a process by which a speech community in a contact situation (i.e. consisting of bi/ multilingual speakers) gradually stops using one of its two languages in favor of the other. The general factors of language shift are socially influenced and determined. This research focused on speakers' attitudes (both explicit and unstated) towards language and domains of language use in the community. In addition, attention was given to the effects of language shift in the context of Kathmandu Valley.

Language shift, sometimes referred to as language transfer or language replacement or assimilation, is the process whereby a speech community of a language shifts to speak another language, usually over an extended period of time. The language shift may have different effect on a language community. There can be religious and cultural shift along with language shift; and some different language may emerge. Language shift is one of the effects of globalization. Nepalese labor migration and market force have a significant effect on language shift in the Sherpa community as workers become acquainted with the languages used in the countries where they are working. As a result, there is language shift. Communication problem may occur even among speakers of the same language if they are of different ages and reside in different places.

Most of the young people of the Newar community interviewed during the fieldwork said that they use Newar language while talking to their older generations, but Nepali when communicating with the younger ones. And, this shift towards Nepali and even English (to some extent) has been reinforced by the growing influence of modern media and technology. The generation gap among the different age groups is reflected in the following remark made by a Newar man (56):

> I myself and my wife like Newar TV programs, but my daughter prefers Hindi serials, she always watches these serials, and our son enjoys sports mostly in English language. (Interview, February 2018)

One important topic in the study of language contact is how it is related to the way that people choose to use one or other language/s from one generation to the next. In this regard, it is important to see whether (and how far) the speakers of new generation are adopting their mother tongue or using additional new languages they have learnt from different contexts. Regarding the pattern of intergenerational shift of this kind, though all the domains of language use are not analyzed here, the domain of personal activities has been considered for a brief analysis.

For example, in the activities of telling stories to children as well as others, people in the age group of 15–25 years did not make use of Newari, though older generations do use Newari for the same purpose. As revealed from personal interviews, members of Newar language community in the age group of 15–25 hardly use Newari words for counting money (*chharka, nirka, sworka, pyarka,* etc.), though older generations very commonly use in these words their daily communication.

However, in some cases, the younger-generation people (15–25 years) were found using the mother tongue in all the personal activities covered by this study. Many Newar speakers use their native tongue in the domains of cultural, religious and some of the formal situations as well. However, data indicates that the younger generation of mother tongue speakers are gradually motivated to move to other "dominant" languages like Nepali and English under the influence of globalization, education, migration, business and communication technologies and the media.

5.5   CAUSES AND IMPACTS OF LANGUAGE CONTACT

This section discusses some major trends of language shifts in Kathmandu Valley, focusing on diverse domains of activities. It also explores the causes and impacts of such shifts in languages spoken by Newar people in Kathmandu Valley. The analysis of FGDs, individual interviews and field observations demonstrate the following causes and impacts.

5.5.1   Causes of Language Contact

5.5.1.1   Media, Migration and Marriage (M3)

The analysis of the data on the Newar-speaking community demonstrates that there are many factors that stimulate language contact. Media, migration and marriage (M3) are found to have vital impact on both contact and shift. Growing consumption of media, no matter whether that be electronic or print, exposes local mother tongue speakers to regional and global languages. As is observed in Nepal's linguistic landscape, the influence of Nepali-, Hindi- and English-medium channels is strong. Such influence may be observed in people's growing consumption of Nepali channels especially for news, entertainment and information about diverse social, cultural and political aspects of the state; Hindi channels appeal especially for entertainment; and English-language channels for entertainment, sports and international/ global exposure. The massive use of many social networking sites because of the availability of internet in computers, pads and smart phones, has widened access to media. Hence, newspaper and social networking sites like Facebook and Twitter, and many other print as well as audiovisual means such as TV channels and FM radios accelerate language contact and shift. Newars living in Kathmandu Valley enjoy access to all sorts of media.

Migration, as pointed out above, is another important cause of language contact and shift. Looking at the 2001 Census, Kathmandu city had almost 42% internal migrants from both rural and urban areas of Nepal (44% migrants if one includes the foreign-born). If intra-district migration were to be considered, the city had more than 50% in-migrants in 2001. Of the total valley immigrants, Kathmandu City received 78.6% of the total rural migrants and 64.8% of the urban migrants from other districts. With the exception of Bhaktapur, the cities of the Kathmandu Valley such as Lalitpur (32%), Madhyapur (27.6%) and Kirtipur (23.2%) have been accommodating an increasing proportion of in-migrants during the last decade. The Newars have not been rapid migrants compared to other ethnic groups in Nepal. However, the migration of many people into Kathmandu Valley has an indirect impact on Newar speakers.

Newar have been affected by the long-term migration of people to Kathmandu Valley in different periods of history. After the unification movement, Khasas migrated to the valley when Prithvi Narayan Shaha became the king of unified Nepal. The 1990 multiparty revolution and 1996 Maoist revolution brought many people to live in Kathmandu Valley permanently, so that the Newar proportion of the Kathmandu Valley population, which was 55% in 1952/1954 fell to around 35% of the total population by 2011. This affected the lifestyle and linguistic and cultural identity of the Newar people.

Language shift that depends on external migration can be observed in personal narratives. For example, a Newar-speaking Maharjan girl (29 yrs.) said had learnt Japanese and English in order to find her future career in Japan. She said,

> *My relatives especially those in Japan use English and Japanese, I also communicate with them in these languages. Since I am planning to go to Japan in my future, I am learning Japanese and using it with my relatives in Japan.* (Interview, Nikki, April 2016)

Such a situation could be observed in the narratives of Rajesh (42 yrs.), a Newar-speaking man who had been in Qatar for the last eight years. He said,

> *We don't find good jobs here, we have to leave for other countries for labor works, so I think we have to learn the languages, so we could adjust there.* (Interview, February 2017)

Nikki and Rajesh's narratives are just some examples among the numerous evidences from the respondents involved in this study. These stories, in one way or another, reveal how language shifts, especially from local languages to regional or global languages, underpin migration.

Marriage is one more cause of migration that often promotes language shift. Interlingual marriage promotes language shift. The story of Kanchan Jha, a 33-year-old Maithili-speaking woman is worthy of reference here. Kanchan, a typical Maithili girl of Siraha district, married a Newar-speaking boy in Kathmandu some seven years back. The early days of her married life were quite inharmonious due to her unfamiliarity with the Newar language. Conflicts increased with her monolingual Newar mother-in-law and other members of her husband's family made her serious in learning the language. Gradually, she started to learn Newari by carefully observing Newar mother tongue users and picking up on the Newar terms for the objects they pointed to. Now she understands Newar languages and culture. Though she speaks Nepali with her husband and other family members she sometimes uses Newar with older relatives. The story of Kanchan typifies many that the researchers encountered in the field. Yet, her case is important in the sense that language shift moved her from one local language (Maithili) to another (Newar) (Interview, Kanchan Jha, March 2017). Unlike Kanchan, Kabita, another Newar-speaking woman's experience demonstrates that her marriage to a Nepali-speaking man ultimately pushed her to shift from Newar to Nepali. Thus, the data indicate that marriage has become an important cause of language shift, mostly in the case of female participants.

5.5.1.2 Education

Education is the most authentic cause of language shift in a multilingual society. Sometimes, a state ideology to expose young citizens to dominant national, regional and international languages promotes language shift, especially in those young citizens. The analysis given here often indicates that Newar is extensively used in its local contexts, but that the language has not been (well) recognized in formal schooling and academic institutions. Some practices of educating young children in their mother tongue have been terminated owing to a lack of public interest, concrete policies on mother tongue education, and a parental desire to educate their children in dominant languages such as Nepali and English. Since "English-prioritized schooling access for the children is often perceived as the symbol of a better future, better social status and economic soundness of the household" (Devkota 2018: 111), parents are more motivated to make their children to learn English and Nepali languages instead of their mother tongue. The use of Newar within the community may be dominant but education policy has made Newar an optional language, which results in language shift.

In the Newar-dominant community of Kathmandu Valley, informants often explained how their children have been extensively exposed to Nepali and English languages in place of their mother tongue. Badri Lal Maharjan (75 yrs.) from a typical Newar-speaking community said,

> *In the distant past, there was provision of Newar language subject in school curricula along with Nepali and English, but now schools don't teach that, our children do not study Newar language anywhere formally, they learn Nepali and even more English instead, so how they could learn Newar language?* (Interview, February, 2018)

In FGDs that were carried out in three major areas of Kathmandu Valley, the participants often explained how their children have been extensively exposed to Nepali and English languages in place of their mother tongue. Harshaman (45 yrs.) from the typical Newar-speaking community of Bhajangal, Kirtipur said,

> *There were teachers who used to teach and explained in Newar in our local schools to the children, but now schools don't teach in that way, our children do not study and speak Newar language anywhere formally, they learn Nepali and even more English instead, so how they could save Newari language?* (Interview, January, 2018)

Rati Maharjan (38 yrs.) points out how educational practices have become more market-oriented and young children are automatically detached from their mother tongues in favor of learning languages which are more powerful in the job/ labor market. As she narrated,

> *my children don't use Newar, only old people use, they don't have to read and write it [Newar] at schools, schools expect them speak more Nepali and English, so they now are good at Nepali and English, not in Newar at all.* (Interview, July, 2017)

These personal narratives indicate that schooling/ education is crucial in promoting and shaping language shift. Schools' emphasis on more dominant state or global language ultimately detaches young people from their mother tongue. This indicates that a national language policy may effect a shift in language in the long term.

5.5.1.3 Travel and Tourism

Kathmandu Valley is not only linguistically and culturally diverse, but also ecologically and geographically distinct. Due to its diversity in culture as well as its wealth of unique historical and religious monuments, Kathmandu Valley attracts more than half of Nepal's tourists. Every year, thousands of people from around the world visit Nepal. Some of them are on holiday, while some want to study the languages and cultures of the people and the country's natural resources. For all these visitors, whatever their national languages may be, English plays a significant role as a medium of communication, from booking tickets and hotels to arranging travel and trekking.

Newar culture and its diverse traditions are the most important attractions for tourists visiting Nepal. The Hanuman Dhoka Durbar Square, Patan Durbar Square and Bhaktapur Durbar Square are the richest cultural and historical heritage of Kathmandu Valley. On the other hand, Kumari and other cultural festivals of the valley are the center of attractions to all kinds of people in Kathmandu. All stakeholders associated with the travel and tourism industry, such as hotel, restaurant and trekking entrepreneurs, must have knowledge of English, Nepali and Hindi in order to communicate with tourists. Not all everyone involved in this business is highly educated. Some are illiterate and run small lodges and restaurants in their respective areas and automatically develop competence in foreign languages like English, Hindi and Chinese through direct contact with foreigners. Thus, travel and tourism is one of the important factors of language contact and shift from local language to many foreign languages.

5.5.1.4 Market Forces and Economic Benefits

Language is directly connected to contemporary market and business activities. Traditionally, Newar were renowned for doing different business, moving from place to place. Now the situation in Kathmandu Valley has drastically changed. People from different linguistic and economic backgrounds have migrated and live there permanently for business and other purposes. This research found a number of examples in diverse study sites where people are using and shifting their language for business and economic reasons.

A businessman (Ravi, 47 yrs.) at Patan said,

Bolna ta aafnai bhasa man parchha tara k garnu business le garda Nepali, English ra Hindi badhi bolinchha.aba ta chhora chori haru pani hamro bhasa bolna chhode [*I like to speak my own language but I have to speak Nepali, English or Hindi otherwise people do not come to my shop*]. (Interview, 2018)

The story of Ravi can be seen as characteristic of language shift guided by market forces, particularly by business.

Market forces are seen to be imperative in language shift in different ways. The growing trend of emigration of Nepali citizens to international labor markets such as the Gulf and other Western countries requires them to learn a particular language(s) that benefits them in the new social context; no matter that it is predominantly for instrumental purposes in the beginning. Language shift ultimately ensues. A Newari-speaking man (38) from Bhaktapur commented,

Where are our languages, I mean Newar, Tamang, Gurung?... in media we listen to Nepali and English, even Hindi rather than our local languages, we read English, Nepali, Hindi ... in the advertisements and manuals of materials we buy at home ... we have to go to other countries for work or study, so what happens if we don't learn these languages?

Such comments by participants clearly demonstrate why people are motivated to acquire languages such as Nepali in the national context, and English or other dominant languages under the influence of current market and economic policy.

The movement of people also has to be taken into account when analyzing the linguistic situation in Nepal. People have to migrate for jobs, trade and communications. Thus, rural Nepalese who moved to such cities as Kathmandu have been shifted to urban identities, with associated use of new languages in their new context. They feel proud of being permanent residents of a big city such as Kathmandu.

5.5.1.5 Political-Ideological Intervention
Political-ideological intervention of the state is another powerful factor in promoting language shift through contact. The 1959 and 1962 Constitutions of Nepal confer the status of national language on Nepali.

During the past century, Nepali has taken great strides to raise itself to the status of the national language. Although studies on the comprehension and the use of Nepali by non-Nepali speakers are few and far between, sheer expediency seems to have driven more and more non-Nepali speakers to use and understand it in their day-to-day transactions, interethnic communications and, above all, in their dealings with the channels of the local and national administration. Since the very instigation of modern Nepal, the Nepali language has been highlighted as the language of unity, the language of social harmony and national integration. In addition, Nepali has been intensively employed in schooling/ education, media and formal communication in the state. Such intervention has promoted the Nepali language throughout the nation.

Due to the lack of a concrete plan by the Nepalese government regarding the development of ethnic languages, the English language, along with Nepali, has become predominant in school curricula, both in rural and urban parts of Nepal. The learning of English provides Nepalese with opportunities to obtain jobs in various national and international governmental organizations and in the media. Therefore, a large section of the Nepalese people is attracted to the English language more than other local languages.

As has been explored in the interviews and FGDs, the growing shift to Nepali and English language is because of their extensive use and applicability in formal situations, media, education and other formal fields. Narratives of respondents from diverse socioeconomic backgrounds demonstrate that their shifts to Nepali and English language are mostly related to fulfilling pragmatic purposes.

5.5.2   Impacts of Language Contact

5.5.2.1   Ideological/Attitudinal Impact

Language has a crucial role in the ideological process. It is the linking element between individuals' knowledge of the world and their social practices, since it mediates individual thought and behavior. This study demonstrates how Sherpa language reflects ideology and can thus be used not only as a means of communication, but also as an instrument of power and control. The linguistic texture of urban areas in the world can be described as a combination of regional majority languages, a wide range of migrant languages, foreign languages which are learnt by considerable parts of school population, and English as the actual lingua franca in many domains of life (Blommaert 2010). This study points out certain impacts of language contact and shift among the users of the Newar language. As the data demonstrate, the use of mother tongues is concentrated in households and the immediate surrounding communities in religious and cultural activities. Nonetheless, there exists a significant generation gap in the language used in such activities. The younger generations of this language community use Nepali and English language more than they use the mother tongue, that is Newar, in these domains. People often relate their mother tongue to their ethnic identity and highlight its importance for maintaining communal solidarity (CS). However, they relate their shift to Nepali and English language to more pragmatic/ instrumental values including intercultural contacts.

The educated Newars of Kathmandu Valley seek a "better place" even outside Nepal and target foreign countries (especially North America, Australia, Europe, etc.), usually under the influence of neoliberalism. Neoliberalism, which now has influenced all of the dimensions of social experiences, is defined as a theory of political economic practice that proposes human wellbeing can best be advanced by liberating individual entrepreneurial freedoms and skills within an institutional framework characterized by strong private property rights, free markets and free trade (Harvey 2005: 21). This highly market-oriented ideology, which minimizes government interference encourages infinite competition between individuals such that they believe that their current socioeconomic status is completely of their own making (Warriner 2015). This ideology has clearly had some influence on perhaps 60% of the Newar speakers living Kathmandu Valley.

5.5.2.2 Motivational Impact

As discussed earlier, people are more motivated to learn the languages of wider communication (in terms of population and space) instead of the home language for the purpose of communicating outside as well as for formal purposes, occasions and circumstances. While using the mother tongue at home and with family, Newar people have the feeling that their language is for regulating their own cultural and religious activities. Despite this, they raise question over the practical relevance of their mother tongue in formal, official and administrative situations. In many circumstances, people were found not to believe in the possibilities of making use of their mother tongue for the purposes of educational, administrative and similar formal works. In the case of Newar language, the respondents often specified Nepali as the language for formal activities and contact with the people of other mother tongues. As a result of the shift from Newari to Nepali, it is possible that there will be a gradual increase in the number of people who have Nepali as their mother tongue, especially in the urban areas like Kathmandu. As the use of local language diminishes in formal situations and activities, people have the tendency of thinking that Nepali occupies a higher position than their local mother tongue. This sort of feeling can be found even though they use the local mother tongue at home and within limited social surroundings.

5.6 Summary

This chapter has discussed various domains of language use and attitudes based on the data collected through questionnaires, FGD and interviews. The data and analysis show that mother tongue is heavily used in cultural and religious activities, but Nepali is dominantly used in social, official, ceremonial and media-related activities. English and Hindi languages are used in media, ceremonial and official activities. The influence of English is much greater than Hindi among Newar people, which indicates the influence of globalization and Western traditions. Newars have been directly involved in official and academic activities as well as tourism, which motivate them to deal with many foreigners in English and Nepali rather than other languages. A shift in a language often brings about a shift in identity, though there may be resistance to adopting a new language. A new language and the new identity may be actively promoted or persuaded. Newar living in the capital city have been influenced directly and indirectly by the globalization and international linkage and communication. Moreover, they have been involved in various social, cultural and ceremonial activities within the new mixed society which motivates them to shift into new target languages from the ancestral source language. In this context, this study is connected with the sociopolitical factors/ variables where different language communities/ speakers share different contexts and situations. Existing political, social and economic factors contribute to language use and attitude. Nepali and English languages are becoming more valuable and influential in the Newar-speaking community, Nepali being the dominant language in the capital city as well as the lingua franca of the country and English being the international language for various purposes. Both are carrying the threat of language shift and endangerment.

NOTE

1. Official name recognized by the Government of Nepal.

BIBLIOGRAPHY

Blommaert, J. (2010). *The sociolinguistics of globalization*. Cambridge and New York: Cambridge University Press.

Central Bureau of Statistics. (2011). *Population of Nepal*. Kathmandu: National Planning Commission.

Devkota, K. R. (2018). Navigating exclusionary-inclusion: Experience of Dalit school children in rural Nepal. *Globe: Journal of Language, Culture and Communication, 6*, 106–120. Alborg: Alborg University Press.

Gautam, B. L. (2018). Language shift in Newar: A case study in the Kathmandu valley. *Nepalese Linguistics, 33*(1), 33–42.

Gautam, B. L. (2020). *Language contact in Kathmandu*. An unpublished PhD dissertation, Tribhuvan University, Kathmandu.

Harvey, D. (2005). *A brief history of neoliberalism*. Oxford: OUP.

Malla, K. P. (2015). *From Literature to culture: Selected writings on Nepalese studies, 1980–2010*. Kathmandu: Social Science Baha.

Nepali, G. S. (1965). *The Newars: An ethno-sociological study of a Himalayan community*. Bombay: United Asia Publications.

Warriner, D. S. (2015). "Here, without English, you are dead" Ideologies of languages and discourses of neoliberalism in adult English language learning. *Journal of Multilingual and Multicultural Development, 37*(5), 495–508. Taylor and Francis.

CHAPTER 6

Language Contact in Maithili

6.1   Introduction

This chapter looks at the patterns of language use in different aspects of language contact in the Maithili speech community residing in the Kathmandu Valley. It consists of five sections: Sect. 6.1 introduces the Maithili language, including its demographic profile in the Kathmandu Valley; Sect. 6.2 sheds light on the patterns of language use; Sect. 6.3 assesses the language contact and intergenerational shift in the Maithili speech community living in Kathmandu Valley; Sect. 6.4, analyzes the causes and impacts of language contact from ideological perspectives; finally, Sect. 6.5 summarizes the findings from the discussion.

6.1.1   *The Maithili Language and Its Demographic Profile*

In this section, a brief introduction of the Maithili language is presented, then its demographic profile is given.

6.1.1.1 *The Maithili Language*
Maithili is an Indo-Aryan language spoken in Nepal and India. The term Maithili is derived from Mithila, the prehistoric ancient kingdom ruled by King Janak and the birthplace of *Janaki*[1] or Sita. This region was also called Tairabhukuti, the ancient name of Tirahut comprising both Darbhanga and Muzaffarpur districts of Bihar, India, and the language spoken in this

B. L. Gautam, *Language Contact in Nepal*, https://doi.org/10.1007/978-3-030-68810-3_6

region was also known as Tirhutiya. The Maithili language has alternative names such as *Apabhramsa, Bihari, Dehati, Maitili,,Tirahutia* and *Tirhuti*, and has a number of dialects such as *Bajjika, Bantar, Barei, Barmeli, Dehati, Kawar, Kyabrat, Makrana, Musar, Tati* and *Thenthi* (Eppele et al. 2012: 47). Maithili also flourished as a court language in Kathmandu Valley during the Malla period. Several literary works (especially dramas and songs) and inscriptions in Maithili are still preserved at the National Archive in Kathmandu.

The Maithili-speaking area is popularly known as Mithilaland. Most of it is located in Bihar state of northern India. It includes a large area of the plains of north Bihar. It extends to the central and eastern part of the Tarai region of Nepal. Tradition holds that Mithila is bounded on the north by the Himalayan foothills, and in the south, east, and west by the Ganges, Kosi, and Gandaki rivers respectively (Jha 1958: 1). The language borders, though, according to reports by many educated Maithili speakers, do not match the traditional eastern, western and southern boundaries. On the west the Maithili area does not extend all the way to the Gandak, but ends somewhere in the vicinity of the town of Muzaffarpur. In the east it extends past the Kosi to somewhere in the western part of Purnia district. The Maithili-speaking area also extends south of the Ganges and is spoken in large parts of the districts of Munger and Bhagalpur. It is spoken in the districts of Morang, Sunsari, Saptari, Siraha, Dhanusha, Mahottari, Sarlahi, and Rautahat of Nepal; and Madhubani, Darbhanga, Sitamarhi, Saharsa, Madhepura, Purnea, East-Muzaffarpur, Samastipur, Vaishali, and Begusarai districts of Bihar state. Maithili is bordered on the south by Magahi, the language to which it is most closely related. To the west its neighbor is Bhojpuri; to the east, Bengali; and to the north, Nepali (Hugoniot 1997: 35).

Maithili is spoken by a wide variety of castes, both "high" and "low" in the Terai region, and by people of all ages. In Mithila, especially, the Brahmin caste has always been associated with a superior form of Maithili dialect. A large part of this study focuses on the differences in speech between castes. The comparisons made are bilateral between Brahmin speech and the speech of members of various non-Brahmin castes. The linguistic significance of caste in the Maithili milieu makes such comparisons relevant, if not indispensable, to any sociolinguistic study of the language. This variation is a function of caste/ ethnicity of Maithili speakers, their religion, literacy, and occupation.

Maithili language and literature composed in the Kathmandu Valley is characterized by various features such as language contact, multilingualism and migration, in particular, of "political refugees, Brahmans, pundits, men of letters, etc. who while coming from various parts of northern India, streamed by far in the largest number from the northern Indian regions of Bihar and Bangal" (Brinkhaus 1987: 112). In the present context there have been literary writings in all literary genres, especially poetry, plays, and fiction, from both Indian and Nepalese writers. Apart from literature, Maithili writers have also been contributing to other fields like culture, history, journalism and linguistics. In addition to written texts, Maithili has an enormous stock of oral literature in the forms of folktales in prose and verse, ballads and songs. Among them, the ballads of Ras Lila (expressing the love between Radha and Krishna) and Salhes (a prehistoric king) are well-known specimens.

In both Nepal and India, Maithili is a subject of study from school to university level of education. Especially in India, however, it has been adversely affected owing to the lack of official recognition as a medium of instruction. In Nepal, constitutional provision has been made for introducing all the mother tongues spoken in Nepal, including Maithili, as media of instruction at the primary level of education.

Maithili has been taught as a subject in some of schools in Dhanusha, Mahottari, Siraha and Saptari districts and the Curriculum Development Centre (CDC) has also published some textbooks in Maithili from Grade 1 to Grade 5. It has also been taught as an optional subject in Grades 9 and 10. Maithili is also taught as such in the Indian universities of Kolkata, Patna, Bihar, Bhagalpur, Mithila and Benares, and the Tribhuvan University and Nepal Sanskrit University of Nepal. In some older literature "Tirahutia" is an alternative name for Maithili. This name, however, is seldom encountered today.[2]

6.1.2   Demography and Distribution

The number of Maithili speakers in Nepal at the time of the 2011 Census was 3,092,530 which constituted 11.7% of the total population of Nepal and ranks second, exceeded only by the Nepali language (Census, 2011). Maithili is spoken in Nepal, mainly in the eastern Terai region, and India, mainly in the northeastern part of Indian state of Bihar and in adjoining Indian states like West Bengal, Maharashtra and Madhya Pradesh (CBS 2012; Lewis et al. 2013).

Table 6.1 Maithili mother tongue population in different censuses

SN	Census Year	Total Population	Proportion of total population	Total number of languages
1.	1952/1954	1,024,780	12.44%	44
2.	1961	1,130,402	12.10%	36
3.	1971	1,327,242	11.49%	17
4.	1981	1,668,309	11.11%	18
5.	1991	2,191,900	11.85%	32
6.	2001	2,797,582	11.30%	92
7.	2011	3,092,530	11.70%	123

Source: National censuses of Nepal.

Table 6.1 shows the total Maithili population and its share of the total population of Nepal in different past censuses. Analyzing the census data we see that the number of speakers increasing every decade since 1952 but the proportion of Maithili speakers generally decreased after 1952. One significant reason for this has been the increasing number of many other languages like Bajjika in the Terai region from 2001 to 2011 census. There were only 92 languages registered in the 2001 census but there were 123 in 2011.

In the recent times, Maithili speakers have spread to various parts of the world for reasons of employment, education and business. The recent migration of the Maithili people into Kathmandu Valley, and especially the capital city of Nepal is significant from the language contact perspective. The migration seems to have been increasing ever since the 1990 multi-party revolution.

Migration has become a prominent phenomenon in the population dynamics of Nepal. It has been outstripping settlement, which is thought to have had a considerable effect on the decline in fertility. A large proportion of the youth population has been regularly moving abroad. The diaspora population has become a major issue in demographic, social and economic aspects of Nepal.

Kathmandu Valley has become the center for internal migration in Nepal for the last three decades. The reasons behind this are related to socioeconomic, political and geographical conditions. Table 6.2 shows the increase in the Maithili population in Kathmandu Valley.

Table 6.2 shows the massive migration of Maithili people in Kathmandu valley in recent days. From 2001 to 2011 we can see a large amount of

Table 6.2 Maithili population in Kathmandu Valley in two censuses

SN	District	2001			2011			Increment percentage
		Total	Male	Female	Total	Male	Female	
1	Kathmandu	5927	4351	1576	36,929	24,966	11,963	72.36
2	Lalitpur	2290	1627	663	11,905	7976	3929	55.38
3	Bhaktapur	569	401	168	3340	2214	1126	59.1
Grand total		8786	6379	2407	52,174	35,156	17,018	71.17

migrants moving towards Kathmandu valley—72.36% in Kathmandu, 55.38% in Lalitpur and 59.1% in Bhaktapur district. The average increment rate in Kathmandu valley between the two censuses is 71.17%. If we carefully observe the data, we find that the number of male migrants is more than double that of female migrants to the Kathmandu valley. This internal migration has changed the linguistic and cultural demographics of Kathmandu valley and made the capital city truly cosmopolitan.

6.2   DOMAINS OF LANGUAGE USE IN MAITHILI

This section mainly deals with the trends of language shift, focusing on the diverse domains of language use and attitudes among the Maithili language speakers residing in Kathmandu Valley. The different patterns of language use observed in the Maithili speech community are presented in the following sub-sections:

6.2.1   Informal Situations

Informal situations in this study are those situations in which people carry out many activities casually without being conscious of or caring about the people and community outside. There are two types of informal activities Maithili speech community in Kathmandu: behavioral and personal. They are briefly discussed below:

Behavioral activities

Behavioral activities here are activities which show the different psychological behavior of the informants. These include activities such as making friends, reading and writing, making telephone calls, talking with different people, shopping and sitting exams. The domains of language use in different behavioral activities are presented in Table 6.3.

Table 6.3 Domains of language use in behavioral activities

Domains	Languages				
	Maithili	Nepali	English	Hindi	Others
1. Making friends	77.77%	71.11%	24.44%	35.55%	2.22%
2. Reading/ writing	17.77%	84.44%	57.77%	2.22%	
3. Getting job	17.77%	73.33%	51.11%	4.44%	2.22%
4. Making telephone calls	77.77%	75.55%	22.22%	28.88%	
5. Shopping	60.00%	86.66%	6.66%	42.22%	2.22%
6. Passing exam	2.44%	71.11%	44.44%	6.66%	
7. Talking with workers	66.66%	64.44%	1.11%	40.00%	
8. Talking with teachers/ professors	15.55%	82.22%	51.11%	4.44%	2.22%
9. Talking with academics	26.66%	86.66%	44.44%	17.7%7	2.22%

Sources: Gautam (2020)

Table 6.3 shows that Nepali language is used in most of the domains in comparison to Maithili, English and Hindi. The influence of English is much higher than that of Hindi because of education, globalization and tourism among the Maithili people living in Kathmandu Valley. Maithili is heavily used for making friends, telephone calls and talking with workers rather than in other activities. Surprisingly, the use of English is very high for reading and writing, sitting exams, getting jobs and talking with teachers and academics.

Personal activities

Personal activities here means those activities which are connected to the personal and interpersonal behaviors of the informants. They include activities such as joking, singing, praying, bargaining, abusing and telling stories.

Table 6.4 shows the different patterns of language use in personal activities.

As presented in the table above, Maithili, Nepali and Hindi languages are used in most of the activities like joking, singing, praying, bargaining with higher frequency than English and other languages. Here the use of English is very low because these are informal personal activities.

The patterns of language used in various personal activities among the Maithili speaking community in Kathmandu Valley is presented in Fig. 6.1.

Figure 6.1 shows that the use of Maithili, Nepali and Hindi in Kathmandu Valley is simultaneous in most of the personal activities like singing, praying, telling stories, village gatherings and meetings. However, the use of English seems to be limited to very few activities like joking, discussing and singing.

Table 6.4 Domains of language use in personal activities

Activities		Language				
		Maithili	*Nepali*	*English*	*Hindi*	*Others*
1.	Joking	73.33%	53.33%	4.44%	13.33%	2.22%
2.	Singing inside	17.77%	15.55%	2.55%	86.66%	
3.	Singing outside	15.55%	20.00%	2.55%	84.44%	4.44%
4.	Praying	62.55%	31.11%	2.55%	24.44%	
5.	Counting	42.55%	53.33%	26.66%	4.44%	
6.	Discussing/ debating	62.55%	66.66%	4.44%	13.33%	2.55%
7.	Quarrelling	64.44%	55.55%	6.66%	6.66%	
8.	Bargaining	40.00%	77.77%		24.44%	
9.	Abusing	73.33%	51.11%	4.44%	8.88%	2.55%
10.	Telling stories to children	68.88%	51.11%	2.55%	6.66%	
11.	Telling stories to other	55.55%	64.44%	4.44%	4.44%	
12.	Family gathering	77.77%	13.33%	2.55%		2.55%
13.	Village/community meeting	57.77%	51.11%		2.55%	

Source: Gautam (2020)

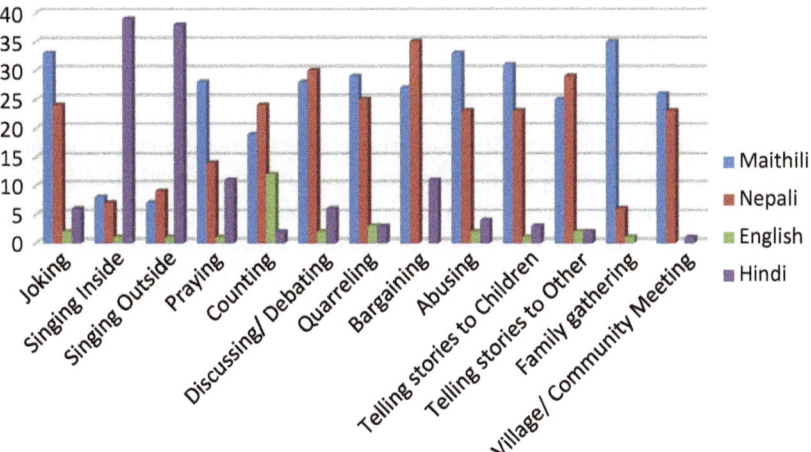

Fig. 6.1 Language use in personal activities. (Source: Gautam 2020)

6.2.2   Formal Situations/ Activities

Formal situations are those activities in which people use various languages and carry out different activities in a formal and official way. These situations involve the workplace, political gathering, public activities, administrative activities and talking with strangers. The table below shows the use of language among Maithili mother-tongue speakers in the domain of formal situations/ activities.

As presented Table 6.5, Nepali is highly dominant compared to Maithili in formal situations and activities. In the activities related to office/ workplace, political/ social gatherings and many public activities in workplaces, Maithili is often use but not as often as Nepali. Maithili is notable in public activities and social gatherings, but occupies no space at all in administrative work. English and Hindi are also occasionally used by Maithili speakers. However, English is more influential than Hindi in formal situations/ activities. The same patterns of language use are presented in Fig. 6.2.

Figure 6.2 indicates the language shifting pattern towards Nepali and other languages from Maithili in city areas. From the data, we can see the heavy use of Nepali language in almost all situations and some use of Hindi and English.

6.2.3   Religious and Cultural Activities

Religious and cultural activities are those which are observed and performed by Maithili people in order to show and preserve their religious and cultural values. These activities include birth ceremonies, marriage ceremonies and religious and cultural festivals. Table 6.6 shows the use of language among Maithili mother-tongue speakers in various religious and cultural activities.

Table 6.5   Domains of language use in formal activities

Activities	Languages			
	Maithili	Nepali	English	Hindi
1. Office/ workplace	17.77%	77.77%	28.88%	4.44%
2. Political/ social gathering	31.11%	73.33%	8.88%	15.55%
3. Public activities/ fun fair	40.00%	75.55%	4.44%	11.11%
3. Administration	4.44%	88.88%	6.66%	4.44%
5. Strangers	37.77%	82.22%	6.66%	24.44%

Source: Gautam (2020)

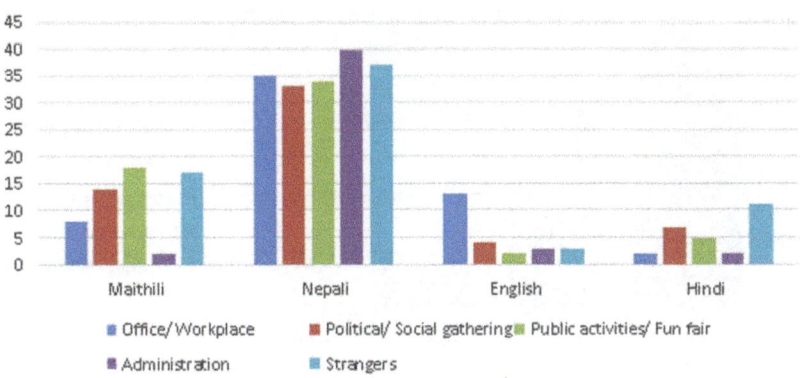

Fig. 6.2 Domains of language use in formal situations. (Source: Gautam 2020)

Table 6.6 Domains of language use in religious/cultural activities

Activities		Languages			
		Maithili	*Nepali*	*Hindi*	*English*
1.	Religious festivals	84.44%	22.22%	2.22%	
2.	Cultural programs	66.66%	60.00%	11.11%	
3.	Death ceremonies	86.66%	22.22%	13.33%	2.22%
4.	Marriage ceremonies	86.66%	28.88%	11.11%	
5.	Birth ceremonies	86.66%	24.44%	8.88%	
6.	Cultural festivals	80.00%	44.44%	17.77%	

Source: Gautam (2020)

Table 6.6 indicates that Maithili is found to be more dominant in religious and cultural activities among Maithili mother-tongue speakers living in Kathmandu Valley. In religious festivals, cultural programs, death rites and rituals, marriage, birth ceremonies and cultural festivals, Nepali also occupies significant space among Maithili mother-tongue speakers. The domains of language use in cultural and religious activities are also presented in Fig. 6.3.

However, as Fig. 6.3 indicates, Nepali is not as widely used as Maithili except in the case of cultural programs. Though, a small influence of Hindi

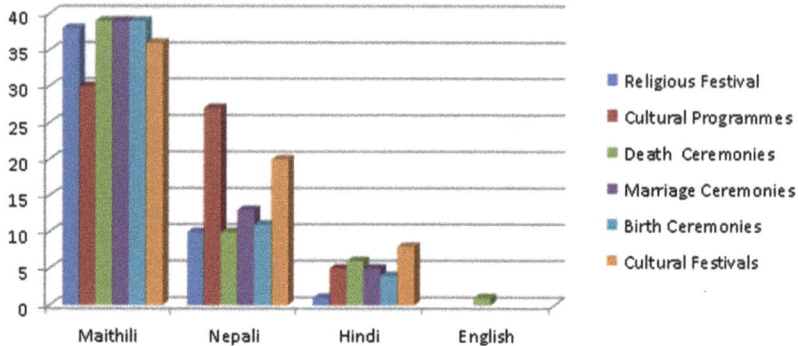

Fig. 6.3 Domains of language use in religious and cultural activities. (Source: Gautam 2020)

can be observed among Maithili mother-tongue speakers, it is less noticeable in religious and cultural activities.

6.2.4   *Family and Friends*

Family and friends are all those people who share culture and day-to-day activities and with whom we share our feelings and opinions through language. The patterns of language use among family and friends in the Maithili-speaking community in Kathmandu Valley are diverse in nature. Table 6.7 demonstrates the use of various languages among Maithili mother-tongue speakers while communicating with family and friends.

Table 6.7 indicates that Maithili is widely used by mother-tongue speakers with family members. Thus, Maithili seems to be dominant while communicating with parents, siblings and spouse. However, Nepali and Maithili are found in use in parallel among the people of this language group while communicating with friends at home as well as outside home.

The patterns of language use within different friends and family members are presented in Fig. 6.4.

Figure 6.4 shows that Hindi and English languages are rarely present in the domain of communicating with family and friends among these speakers. However, Nepali language is predominantly used among friends at home and outside compared to other domains.

Table 6.7 Domains of language use in family and friends

Family and friends	Languages					
	Maithili	Nepali	More Nepali than Maithili	More Maithili than Nepali	Maithili and English	Maithili and Hindi
1. Father	82.22%	2.22%	2.22%	2.22%	–	2.22%
2. Mother	84.44%	2.22%	2.22%	–	–	2.22%
3. Brothers	68.88%	2.22%	8.88%	8.88%	–	2.22%
4. Spouse	46.66%	2.22%	8.88%	6.66%		–
5. Friends at home	33.33%	13.33%	6.66%	24.44%	2.22%	2.22%
6. Friends outside	8.88%	26.66%	8.88%	26.66%	2.22%	2.22%
7. Neighbors at home	33.33%	15.55%	13.33%	17.77%	4.44%	2.22%
8. Neighbors outside	20.00%	26.66%	4.44%	24.44%	4.44%	2.22%

Source: Gautam (2020)

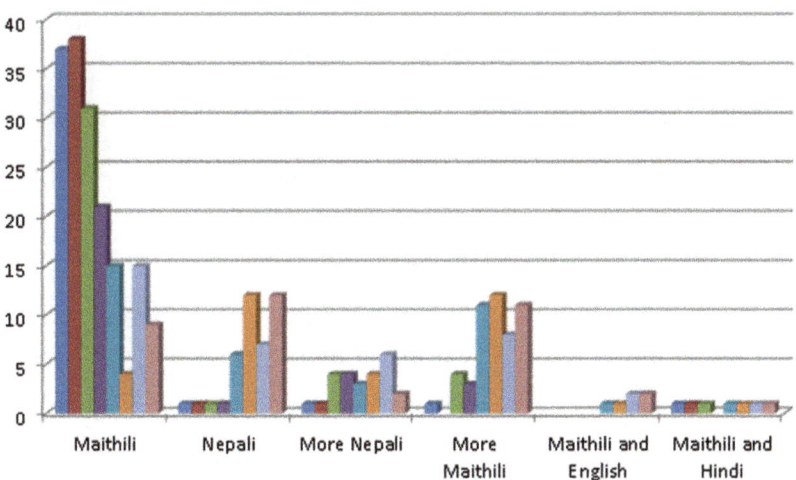

Fig. 6.4 Domains of language use within family and friends. (Source: Gautam 2020)

6.2.5   *Media and Entertainments*

Media and entertainment activities include: listening radio and music, reading newspapers and watching television. Table 6.8 shows the use of language by Maithili mother-tongue speakers in the activities in the domain of media and entertainment.

In the activities listed under media and entertainment, Maithili, Nepali and Hindi occupy significant space among the Maithili mother-tongue speakers. Maithili has been found to occupy notable space in listening to music, listening to news and listening and watching interviews. However, in these domains too, Nepali dominant. The table also shows that Hindi occupies the most influential space in the activities of watching TV serials and listening to music—Nepali is more influential in all the activities including reading newspapers and horoscopes. In addition, the presence of English is noticeable to some extent among Maithili speakers in Kathmandu Valley in the activities of watching TV and reading. The same patterns are presented in Fig. 6.5.

Figure 6.5 indicates the massive use and shift towards Nepali and Hindi language among Maithili speakers living in Kathmandu Valley in media and entertainment related activities. These two languages are highly influential in national and regional media. If this trend continues, Maithili speaking will lose its place in many important domains within few decades.

Table 6.8   Domains of language use in media and entertainment

Activities	Languages			
	Maithili	Nepali	English	Hindi
1. Watching movie/ serial	15.55%	40.00%	22.22%	82.22%
2. Watching news	17.77%	80.00%	15.55%	71.11%
3. Listening to music	37.77%	40.00%	15.55%	84.44%
4. Listening to news	44.44%	75.55%	4.44%	40.00%
5. Listening to interviews	37.77%	77.77%	8.88%	37.77%
6. Reading newspapers	19.99%	80.00%	22.22%	8.88%
7. Reading horoscope	13.33%	71.11%	11.11%	19.99%

Source: Gautam (2020)

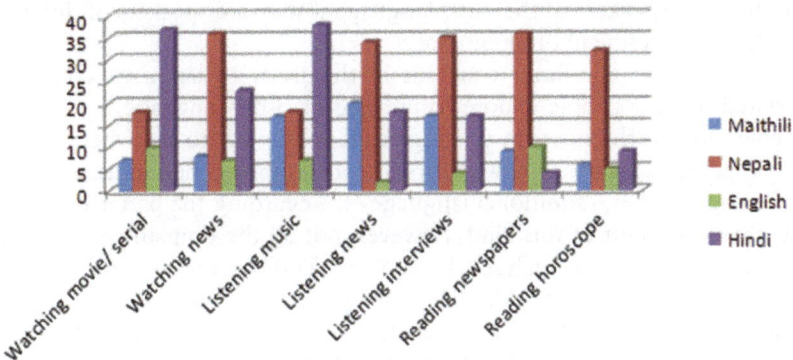

Fig. 6.5 Domains of language use in media and entertainment. (Source: Gautam 2020)

6.3   LANGUAGE CONTACT
AND INTERGENERATIONAL SHIFT

Multilingualism, language contact and language shift are inherent phenomena in Nepal. This study is concerned with language-shifting patterns in the Nepalese context, based on Fishman's Reversing Language Shift (1991). Language shift is the process by which a speech community in a contact situation (i.e. consisting of bi- and/or multilingual speakers) gradually stops using one of its two languages in favor of the other. The causal factors of language shift are generally considered to be social. This study focuses on speakers' attitudes (both explicit and unstated) towards language and domains of language use in the community. In addition, the research focuses on the effects of language shift in the Nepalese context.

Language shift, sometimes referred to as language transfer or language replacement or assimilation, is the process whereby a speech community of a language shifts to speak another language, usually over an extended period of time. Language shift may have different effects on a language community. There may be cultural shift along with language shift; and some different languages can emerge. Language shift is one of the effects of globalization. Nepal's labor migration and market forces have their effect on language shift. Nepal's laborers working in different countries are acquainted with the languages used in those countries. As a result, there is language shift. There might be communication problem as well among the speakers of the same language if they are speakers of different dialects and reside in different places.

One of the significant concerns in the study of language contact is related to how people choose to use one or other language/s from one generation to the next. In this regard, it is relevant to see whether (and how far) the speakers of new generation are adopting their mother tongue or using another/ additional language/s. Regarding the pattern of inter-generational shift of this kind, however, not all the domains of language use and attitude are analyzed here. Some FGD interviews and informal observations among the Maithili language speakers living in Kathmandu Valley are carefully studied and analyzed in this section In Maithili language community It can be observed that the members of the older generation often use the Maithili language whereas it is in merely nominal use by members of younger generations. For example, a Maithili speaker (70) of Siraha living in Kupondole, while talking about intergenerational language shift said,

> *ke garnu sir, haami ta bolchu ni tara aaileka ketaketiharu bolnai mandainan; ajjha boarding padneharu ta Englishma bolcha* [What to do, we speak Maithili but our children do not want to speak this language, even those who go to boarding school speak English instead of Maithili]. (Interview, September 2016)

This is evidence that language is shifting to English among the new generation. The quantitative analysis of Maithili in the previous section shows the same trends as well. For example, in the activities of telling stories to children as well as others, Maithili was not in use in the age group of 15–25 years even though the older generations are using it for the same purpose.

However, in some cases, the younger generation people (15–25 years) did use the mother tongue in all personal activities when the researcher visited to their home and family in Kathmandu Valley. Maithili speakers have been noticed using their mother tongue in the context of cultural, religious and sometimes in the formal situations as well. However, data indicates that the younger generation of mother-tongue speakers is gradually being motivated to other dominant languages like Nepali, Hindi and English because of the impact of globalization, business and communication as well as new technologies and the media.

6.4   Causes and Impacts of Language Contact

This section deals with some major trends of language contact in Kathmandu, centering on different domains of activities spoken by Maithili people living in Kathmandu Valley. The analysis of FGDs, individual interviews and field observations exhibit the following causes and impacts.

6.4.1   Causes of Language Contact

Media, Migration and Marriage (M3)

The data collected from questionnaires, FGD and individual interviews demonstrate that there are many causes that encourage language contact in the Maithili-speaking community. Media, migration and marriage (M3) are observed as major causes of contact and shift. Growing number of media and increasing consumption of many media genres, both electronic and print, exposes local mother tongue speakers to regional and global languages. As observed in the linguistic landscape of Kathmandu Valley, Nepali-, Hindi- and English-medium TV channels dominate society. Such influence can be observed in growing consumption of Nepali channels especially for news, entertainment and information about the various social, cultural and political aspects of the state; of Hindi channels especially for entertainment; and of English channels for entertainment, sports and international/ global exposure. Poonam, a Maithili girl pursuing college education in Humanities and Social Sciences at Tribhuvan University, Kathmandu narrated her experience thus,

> *You know, this is the era of media and technology, I feel I myself spend more time with them, watching news in Nepali channels, Tele Serials in Hindi Channels and when I want to know about the outer world, I watch BBC, CNN, the National Geography and Animal Planet...so I automatically learn English, Hindi and Nepali instead of Maithili... I like my language but does our language (she meant Maithili) have such channels?* (Poonam, Interview, February 2017)

Poonam's comment here indicates how people of diverse local mother tongues shift to other dominant languages not because they dislike their mother tongues, but because of the limited opportunities they have in using and exposing themselves with their mother tongues.

Migration, as pointed out above, is another vital cause of language contact and shift. The jobs of newly settled immigrants are not determined by their qualifications, skills and experiences, but by gaps in local labor markets. So, the main cause of immigration was the need for work, and many work places are, in turn, a reflection of the new multiethnic pattern of urban life which has resulted from local market immigration (Gumperz 1982: 230). Migration has become a prominent phenomenon in the population dynamics of Nepal. Emigration has been outstripping entry, which is thought to have had a considerable effect on the decline in fertility. The emigration rate, the number of emigrants (out-movers) per thousand population stands at 10.77, whereas the immigration rate is estimated to be 0.46 per thousand populations (CBS 2011). This rate has the different impacts on language contact and shift among the people in multilingual cities like Kathmandu.

Nepal has recently experienced widespread internal as well as external migration. Internal migration is largely taking rural villagers to urban (cities) and semi-urban areas under the influence of education, employment, development, health and other modern facilities. External migration is active in moving population from Nepal to the Middle East, to the Gulf countries including Qatar, Dubai, Kuwait, and to Malaysia and South Korea, as well as to European and American countries, either for earning, or getting higher education, or some other business purposes. In a long term, these moves result in language shift and decay. As this analysis points out, internal migration has provided the space for promoting language shift from local languages to Nepali, English and Hindi for the people living in Kathmandu Valley.

Language shift that depends on external migration can be observed in personal narratives. For example, a Maithili speaking Yadav girl (Deepa, 26 yrs.) said she had learnt Japanese and English languages in order to find her future career in Japan. She said,

my relatives especially those in Japan use English and Japanese, I also communicate with them in these languages. Since I am planning to go to Japan in my future, I am learning Japanese and using it with my relatives in Japan.
(Interview, April 2016)

Such a situation could be observed in the narratives of Rajesh (42 yrs.), a Maithili speaking man who had been living in Qatar for the last eight years. He said,

We don't find good jobs here, we have to leave for other countries for labor works, so I think we have to learn the languages, so we could adjust there. (Interview, March 2017)

Here, Deepa and Rajesh's narratives as such are just some examples among the large-scale evidences from the respondents involved in this study. These stories, in one or another way, suggest us how language shifts especially from local languages to regional or global languages deeply underpin migration.

Marriage is another important cause of migration that often encourages language shift. Marriage between people of inter-lingual background is quite authoritative to understand in how it promotes language shift. The case of Kanchan Jha, described in Section 5.5.1, is instructive. Unlike Kanchan, Sony, a Maithili-speaking woman, had an experience demonstrating that her marriage to a Hindi-speaking man ultimately pushed her to shift from Hindi to Maithili. Thus, the data and the stories indicate that marriage has become an important cause of language shift mostly in the case of female participants of Maithili people in the context of Nepal.

Education

Education plays the most important role in language contact and shift in multilingual society. Sometimes, people are compelled to follow the state's ideology that insists on exposing young citizens to more dominant national, regional and international languages, which promotes language shift especially in young citizens. This analysis often indicates that Maithili explored in this study is extensively used in its local contexts. However, the language has not been (well) recognized in formal schooling and academic institutions. Even some practices of educating young children in their mother tongue have not been appropriately materialized due to the lack of public interest, concrete policies on mother-tongue education, and parental desire to expose their children with more dominant languages such as Nepali, Hindi and English.

In FGDs carried out in three major areas of Kathmandu Valley, the participants often explained how their children have been extensively exposed to Nepali and English languages in place of their mother tongue. Sanjeev Singh (45 yrs.) from a typical Maithili-speaking community said,

In the very past, there were teacher who used to teach and explained in Maithili in our local schools to the children, but now schools don't teach in that way, our children do not study Maithili language anywhere formally, they learn Nepali

and even more English instead, so how they could learn Maithili language?
(Interview, January 2018)

Dilip Shah (58 yrs.) points out how the current educational practices have become more market-oriented and young children are automatically detached from their mother tongue for learning the languages which are more powerful in the job/labor market. As he narrated,

> *Our children don't use Maithili, only old people use, they don't have to read and write it [Maithili] at schools, schools expect them speak more Nepali and English, so they now are good at Nepali and English, not in Maithili at all.*
> (Interview, March 2017)

Both of these personal narratives indicate that schooling/ education is crucial in promoting and shaping language contact and shift. Schools' emphasis on a more dominant state or global language ultimately detaches young people from their mother tongue.

Travel and Tourism

Travelling is another factor in language contact and change, as people move from one place to another. Nepal is a beautiful country with great linguistic and cultural diversity. People visit Nepal for various purposes. In recent years, religious tourists from India, and Sri Lanka are increasing in number because of the attractive religious destinations like Pashupatinath, Janakpur and Lumbini. This has created an opportunity for the people to learn and speak the languages like English, Hindi and Chinese in order to get a job in tourism industry. Thousands of tourists visit Nepal each year and there is an increasing attraction among the youth and educated people to work in travel and tourism-related jobs. Some of them are on holiday, while some of them want to study the languages and cultures of the people. For all of those visitors, whatever their national languages are, English plays a significant role as a medium of communication, from booking tickets and hotels to arranging travel and trekking during their stay in Nepal.

People associated with the travel and tourism industry, such as hotel, restaurant and trekking entrepreneurs, must have knowledge of English in order to communicate with tourists. Not all people involved in this business are highly educated. Some are illiterate and run small lodges and restaurants on their respective areas. They spontaneously develop competency in foreign languages such as English, Hindi, and Chinese. through direct contact with foreigners. Thus, travel and tourism is one of the important causes of language contact and shift from local language to many foreign languages. These days many Maithili people are involved in promoting Mithila arts and culture through tourism to the rest of the world.

Market Forces and Economic Benefits

Market forces are an affective factor intimately connected to the economic benefit of individuals. This study exhibits a number of examples from diverse study sites where people are using and shifting their language because of business and economic purpose. For example, a furniture shop owner (56 yrs.) from Bagbazaar whose mother tongue is Maithili said,

> *ke chha ki, ma ta sabai bhasa bolchhu ra bujhchhu pani.ma Nepali, Hindi, Maithili, English, Urdu ra ali ali Newar pani bolxu. Yo pashal ma bhasa jane pachhi nikkai sajilo hune rahexa.* [I speak and understand many languages. Knowing languages in this profession is good to attract customers]. (Interview, Narendra 2016)

People use language for business purpose rather than their own interest sometimes. Similarly, another businessman (Ricky, 42 yrs.) at Balkhu said,

> *Bolna ta aafnai bhasa man parchha tara k garnu business le garda Hindi ra Nepali badhi bolinchha.aba ta chhora chori haru pani hamro bhasa bolna chhode* [I like to speak my own language but I have to speak Hindi or Nepali otherwise people do not come to my shop]. (Interview 2018)

The comments of both of these participants show how language shift is guided by market forces particularly business.

In multilingual cities like Kathmandu, spreading market and business techniques force language contact and shift. The growing trend of external migration of Nepali people into international labor markets encourages them to learn a particular language(s) that benefits them in a particular social context; no matter that it is extensively for instrumental purposes in the beginning, it ensures language shift ultimately. A Maithili-speaking man (44) in Kathmandu observed,

> *What I think is the current globalization trend has some more effect on the languages we use, for example, I speak Maithili, Nepali and Hindi but I need to learn English so I could find better jobs in the labor market outside the country.* (Interview, February 2018)

Similarly, another Maithili-speaking man (38) from Saptari commented,

Where are our languages, I mean Maithili, Tharu, Bhojpuri...in media we listen to Nepali and English, even Hindi rather than our local languages, we read English, Nepali, Hindi ...in the advertisements and manuals of materials we buy at home...we have to go to other countries for work or study, so what happens if we don't learn these languages?

Such participants' comments clearly hint why people are motivated to learn and use languages such as Nepali in the national context and English or other dominant languages under the influence of current market forces.

The movement of people from one place to another has different meaning for the metalinguistic situation in Nepal. People have to migrate from one place to another for different economic activities like jobs, business, trade or even industrial purposes. Thus, rural Nepalese people displaced to such cities as Kathmandu assume de-ethnicized urban identities. They feel proud of being permanent residents of a big city such as Kathmandu and motivate towards Nepali, English and Hindi rather than their own mother tongue. In this context, it can be said that multiple language ideologies have been working in different people for different contexts. On both a societal and an interpersonal level, the language that a person is able to speak is an index of that person's position in society.

Political-Ideological Intervention

Political-ideological intervention by the state is another significant cause of language shift through contact in Nepal. Previous constitutions of Nepal (1959 and 1962) recognized Nepali as the national language. Although Nepali language had been the court and administrative language for 200 years since the unification movement, its popularity flourished during Panchayat Era (1960–1990). It became the language of power and politics in Nepal. Since the very instigation of modern Nepal, the Nepali language was promoted as the language of unity, social harmony and national integration. Further, Nepali was also intensively employed in schooling/ education, media and formal communication in the state. Such intervention promoted Nepali throughout the nation.

Due to the lack of a concrete plan by the Nepalese government regarding the development of ethnic languages, the English language, along with Nepali, has become predominant in school curricula, both in the rural and urban parts of Nepal. The learning of English provides Nepalese with opportunities to obtain jobs in various national and international governmental organizations and in the media. Therefore, a large section of the Nepalese people is attracted to the English language more than other local languages spoken in Nepal.

As is explored in interviews and FGDs, the growing shift to Nepali, Hindi and English language is because of its widespread use and applicability in the formal situations, media, education and other formal fields in the nation. The narratives of respondents belonging to diverse socioeconomic backgrounds demonstrate that their shifts from Maithili to Nepali, Hindi and English languages are mostly related to fulfilling pragmatic purposes.

6.4.2   Impacts of Language Contact

Ideological/Attitudinal Impact

The main notion that differentiates studies of language ideology from either language attitude or identity is the attitudinal aspect. Language has a crucial role in the ideological process. It is the linking element between individuals' knowledge of the world and their social practices, since it mediates individual thought and behavior. This study intends to demonstrate how the Maithili language reflects ideology and can thus be used not only as a means of communication, but also as an instrument of power and control. The linguistic texture of urban areas in the world can be described as a combination of regional majority languages, a wide range of migrant languages, foreign languages which are learnt by considerable parts of school population and English as the actual lingua franca in many domains of life (Blommaert 2010). This study points out certain impacts of language contact and shift among the users of Maithili language. As the data demonstrate, the use of mother tongues is more concentrated in the household and the immediate surrounding communities in their religious and cultural activities. Nonetheless, there exists a significant generation gap in language use in such activities as well. The younger generation of the Maithili language community use Nepali, Hindi and English language more than their heritage language. People often relate their mother tongues with their ethnic identity and highlight its importance for maintaining communal solidarity (CS). However, they relate their shift to Hindi, Nepali and English to more pragmatic/ instrumental values, including intercultural contacts.

Motivational Impact

A set of questions were administered to the informants in order to understand the attitudes towards Nepali language including Maithili. Regarding the item, **"If there are two people coming to work at your** place having same skills and experiences, one speaks Maithili and another speaks Nepali, whom would you choose?" more than half of the informants replied that they choose the one with the mother tongue whereas slightly more than one-third of the informants would accept either (Nepali or mother tongue). This result shows a positive attitude towards the official language of Nepal.

During the interview, the informants were asked for their reasons for choosing languages. The people who chose Maithili said that it is very easy for them to communicate and handle because of cultural and ethnic similarity. They said that language makes people to be close each other while sharing food and language.

On the other hand, some people responded either and they described that the knowledge of the language they know i.e. Nepali or Maithili creates various difficulties in bargaining and working condition (Fig. 6.6).

As discussed earlier, people are more motivated to learn the languages of wider communication (in terms of population and space) instead of the home language while communicating outside as well as for formal purposes, occasions and circumstances. While using the mother tongue at home and with family, Maithili people have the feeling that their language is for

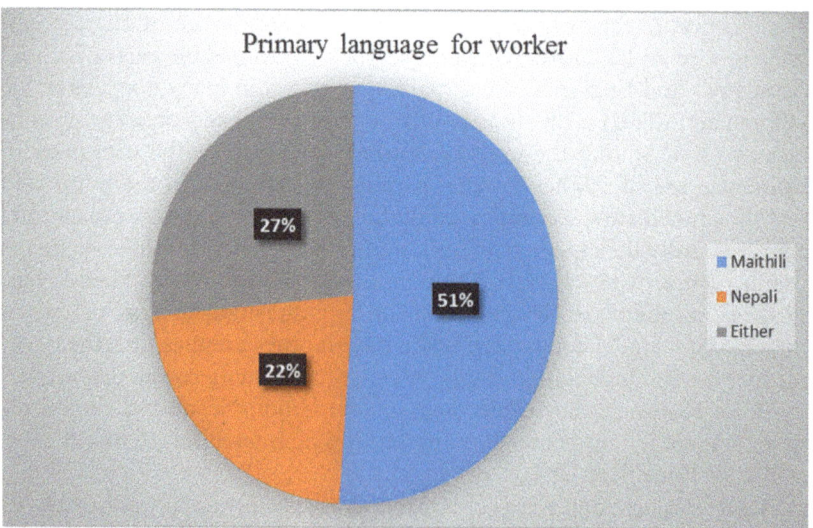

Fig. 6.6   Primary language for workers. (Sources: Gautam 2020)

regulating their own cultural and religious activities. Despite this, they raise questions over the practical relevance of their mother tongue in formal, official and administrative situations as well. In many circumstances, people did not believe in the possibility of using their mother tongue for the purposes of educational, administrative and similar formal works. In the case of the Maithili language, the respondents often specified Nepali as the language for formal activities and contact with the people of other mother tongues. As a result of the shift from Maithili to Nepali, there is a possibility of a gradual increase in the number of Nepali mother tongue speaking people in urban areas like Kathmandu. Since the use of local language is found less in the case of formal situations and activities, people have the tendency to think that Nepali occupies a higher position than their local mother tongues. This sort of feeling can be found even though they use the mother tongue at home and within limited social surroundings.

6.5   SUMMARY

In the study area, it has been noted that the representative respondents of Maithili community mostly use their mother tongue i.e. Maithili in the family, cultural or religious activities, and less for the purpose of outside contact in the marketplace and business. The use of Maithili is less in formal activities including education and administration. In the case of their immediate community or surroundings, there is a tendency to use Maithili as well as a second language, that is. Nepali is found in the field—more or less applicable to the languages. Considering the trend across generations, however, indications of the reduced use of the mother tongue is noticeable among the new generation people. Nonetheless, older generations are maintaining the use of mother tongue in several ways. This shows the various ideological impacts of language contact in the Maithili-language community driving language shift and language death.

Migrated urban areas are very important sites in imposing language dominance, particularly capital cities and trade and commercial centers; towns tend to dominate the surrounding rural areas and their influence radiates out those areas. A shift in a language often brings a shift in identity though there may be resistance to adopting a new language. The new language and the new identity may be actively promoted or persuaded. Migrated Maithili people living in the capital city have been influenced directly and indirectly by globalization and international linkage and communication. Moreover, they have been involved in various social, cultural and ceremonial activities with the new mixed society which motivates them to shift into new target languages from the ancestral source language. In this context, this study is connected with the sociopolitical factors/ variables where different language communities/ speakers share different contexts and situations. So multilingualism in Kathmandu Valley has become an obligatory part of people living in this city. Existing political, social and economic factors contribute to language use and attitude. Nepali, being the dominant language in the capital city, the lingua franca of the country, and Hindi, being the lingua franca of South Asia, are becoming more valuable and influential in the Maithili community, which is an indication of language shift and endangerment.

Notes

1. King Janak's daughter and Lord Ram's wife in *Ramayana*.
2. In this book, it will always be referred to simply as Maithili.

Bibliography

Blommaert, J. (2010). *The sociolinguistics of globalization*. Cambridge and New York: Cambridge University Press.

Brinkhaus, H. (1987). *Pradyumnavijaya-nataka* (of jagatprakashamalla). In *The Pradyumna-Prabhavati legend in Nepal: A study of the Hindu myth of the draining of the Nepal valley* (pp. 161–345). Stuttgart: Franz Steiner, Wiesbaden.

Central Bureau of Statistics. (2011). *Population of Nepal*. Kathmandu: National Planning Commission.

Central Bureau of Statistics. (2012). *National population and housing census-2011*. Kathmandu: Central Bureau of Statistics, National Planning Commission (NPC).

Eppele, J., Paul, L., Regmi, D. R., & Yadava, Y. P. (Eds.). (2012). *Ethnologue: Languages of Nepal*. Kathmandu: Central Department of Linguistics and SIL International.

Fishman, J. A. (1991). *Reversing language shift: Theoretical and empirical foundations of assistance to threatened languages*. Clevedon, UK: Multilingual Matters.

Gautam, B. L. (2020). *Language contact in Kathmandu*. An unpublished PhD dissertation, Tribhuvan University, Kathmandu.

Gumperz, J. J. (1982). *Language and social identity*. Cambridge, UK: Cambridge University Press.

Hugoniot, K. (1997). *A sociolinguistic profile of the dialects of Maithili*. Kathmandu: SIL.

Jha, S. (1958). *The formation of the Maithili language*. London: Luzac & Co..

CHAPTER 7

Language Shift in Nepal

7.1 Introduction

This chapter mainly deals with the trends of language shift, focusing on the diverse domains of language use and impact of language shift in different languages spoken in Nepal. It is based on research carried out with the support of Language Commission Nepal in 2018.Four languages viz. Dotyali, Jumli, Tharu and Nepali have been selected from the data in order to see whether any shift is found among the speakers of these languages from mother tongue into other language/s. The patterns of shift noticed in these languages are depicted under sub-headings that follow where the data are described. Each of the sub-headings are based on the informants' responses regarding the use of language in various activities. This chapter simply describes the various trends and patterns of language shift in Nepal where we can see many different attitudinal aspects of language contact and shift.

7.2 Language Shift in Dotyali

Dotyali is the most widely spoken and understood language in the Far Western Province of Nepal, spoken by 790,000 people (Census, 2011). It is spoken commonly in the districts of Doti, Dadheldhura, Kanchanpur, Bajura, Baitadi, Achham, Bajhang and Kailali. However, Nepali is another dominant and main contact language in this area. The shift from Dotyali

B. L. Gautam, *Language Contact in Nepal*,
https://doi.org/10.1007/978-3-030-68810-3_7

to Nepali, Hindi and English as demonstrated by the data are described under the domains of language use given below.

7.2.1   Social Activities

Figure 7.1 shows the use of Dotyali language by Dotyali mother tongue speakers in different social activities.

The Fig. 7.1 shows that Dotyali is strongly used in the activities of joking and family gathering. However, in the activities of singing outside, counting, praying, discussing and telling stories to others, Nepali is more dominant. In the activities of singing inside, quarrelling, shopping/ marketing and village and community meetings Dotyali and Nepali both are found to be competitive in use. Hindi occupies some space in all personal activities; and English also occupies some space in many of them. The analysis of qualitative data indicates that Hindi lexicons are mixed in the conversation of Dotyali speakers. However, they are not used so strongly as Dotyali and Nepali.

The analysis of narratives shows that cultural and domestic activities are performed in Dotyali whereas Nepali and Hindi are spoken simultaneously with outsiders. Migration has been one of the major reasons for

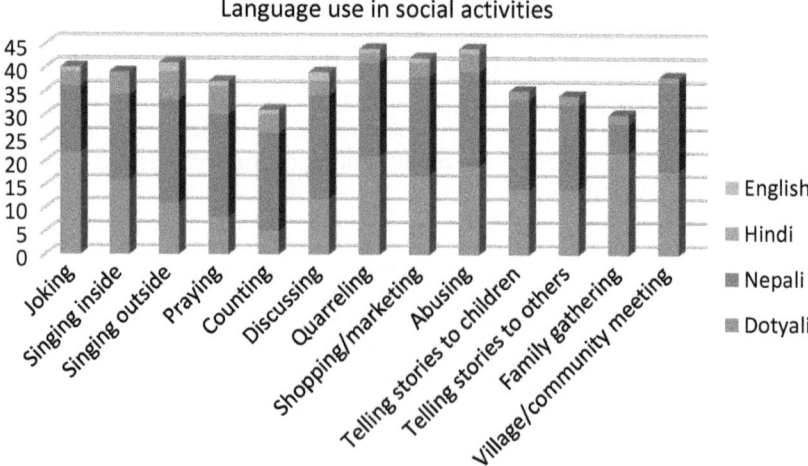

Fig. 7.1 Language use in social activities by Dotyali speakers. (Source: Thapa et al. 2018)

language shift in this area. In this context, for women, marriage has been the reason for migration. A woman (36) originally from Dailekh and living now in Dhangadhi after marriage said,

> "*ma ta Dailekhi bolchhhu tara k garne bihe pachi yaha sabai Dotyali bolchan, tyasaile aba ki Nepali ki Dotyali bhayeko cha mero bhasa.*" [I speak Dailekhi; but after marriage everyone here speaks Dotyali and so either I have to speak Nepali or Dotyali]. (Interview, April 2018)

Dotyali is still much used by elderly people. They still speak Dotyali. But the younger generation is much more attracted towards Nepali due to access it offers to education and business and because of the need to communicate with mixed society in city areas.

7.2.2   Formal Situations/Activities

Table 7.1 shows the use of language among Dotyali mother tongue speakers in different formal situations and activities.

As the table shows, the Nepali language is found to have been used more than Dotyali. English is found to have occupied space in the activities of reading and writing, seeking jobs, sitting exams and talking to teachers/ professors. However, it is less dominant compared to Nepali language. Hindi is used to a small extent but it is less dominant than to Nepali, English and Dotyali in all the activities.

Table 7.1 Use of language in formal situations/ activities (number of respondents)

Formal situations/ activities	Languages used by Dotyali mother tongue speakers				
	Dotyali	Nepali	Hindi	English	Others
Reading and writing	5	17	4	10	–
Seeking jobs	3	16	2	8	–
Sitting exams	1	16	2	11	–
Talking to teachers/ professors	5	17	2	8	–
Talking to intellectuals	5	17	2	3	–
Offices and working places	6	17	1	3	–
Social/political activities	7	16	1	3	–
Public activities and ceremonies	6	17	1	3	–
Administrative activities (document works)	2	17	1	2	–

Source: Thapa et al. (2018)

7.2.3   Media and Entertainment

Media and entertainment is another domain of language use explored in this study. Table 7.2 shows the use of language among Dotyali mother tongue speakers in various domain of media and entertainment activities.

As shown in the table, Dotyali mother tongue speakers use Dotyali, Nepali, and Hindi and English languages. However, Nepali is found as the most dominant language in all the activities mentioned here. Dotyali, though not so strongly used as Nepali, has a remarkable presence in listening to music. The table also indicates that Hindi occupies more space in watching TV serials and listening to music than in other activities, though it is not so dominant as Nepali in these activities. The appearance of English use in all these activities, no matter what extent it is, marks its growing influence among Dotyali mother tongue speakers. The personal stories of Dotyali informants collected during fieldwork also demonstrate that family members of younger generations are much attracted to Nepali and Hindi media including Hindi TV serials.

7.2.4   Religious and Cultural Activities

Table 7.3 shows the language use in religious and cultural activities by Dotyali mother tongue speakers.

As shown in the table, Dotyali language is more dominant than Nepali in religious and cultural activities. Yet, Nepali parallels Dotyali in religious festivals, cultural programs and festivals. Hindi shows very little space in

Table 7.2 Use of language in media and entertainment activities (number of respondents)

Media and entertainment activities	Languages used by Dotyali mother tongue speakers				
	Dotyali	Nepali	Hindi	English	Others
Watching TV serials	6	14	10	3	–
Watching TV news	3	16	8	4	–
Listening to music	10	15	10	4	–
Listening to news	6	17	6	4	–
Listening to and watching interviews	6	17	6	6	–
Reading newspapers	4	17	4	3	–
Reading horoscopes	3	16	5	2	–

Source: Thapa et al. (2018)

Table 7.3 Use of language in religious and cultural activities (number of respondents)

Religious and cultural activities	Languages used by Dotyali mother tongue speakers				
	Dotyali	Nepali	Hindi	English	Others
Religious festivals	15	10	2	–	–
Cultural programs (mass cultural programs)	12	11	2	–	–
Death rites and rituals	17	6		–	–
Marriage ceremonies	17	9	3	–	–
Birth ceremonies	17	6		–	–
Cultural festivals	14	11	2	–	–

Source: Thapa et al. (2018)

Table 7.4 Use of language with family and friends (number of respondents)

Family and friends	Languages used by Dotyali mother tongue speakers				
	Dotyali	Nepali	Hindi	English	Others
Father	17	3	–	–	–
Mother	17	3	–	–	–
Brothers/ sisters	17	9	–	–	–
Spouse	10	6	–	–	–
Friends at home	15	15	–	–	–
Friends outside	7	17	3	4	–

Source: Thapa et al. (2018)

these activities, while English has no presence in any of them at all. Most of the people in this area are Hindu by religion and we see less effect of language shift in these activities.

7.2.5   Family and Friends

Table 7.4 demonstrates language use among Dotyali mother tongue speakers in the domain of family and friends.

As the table shows, the Dotyali language is more dominant while communicating with parents, siblings and spouse in the household environment. It is equal to Nepali while communicating with friends in the home environment. Nepali is more dominant while communicating with friends outside the home. Hindi and English are also used to some extent while communicating with friends outside the home. The dominance of Dotyali language use with family members and friends is demonstrated by some narratives of the users in the field. As commented by a 15-year-old boy,

> *Dotyali is the language that I learnt from my father and mother since the early days of my life; so I enjoy using it while communicating with them. I feel I am closely connected to them if I use Dotyali with them.* (Interview, April 2018)

7.3   LANGUAGE SHIFT IN JUMLI

Jumli is a variety of the Khas Nepali language spoken mainly in Jumla district of Karnali province. It is spoken and understood by many people living in Jumla, Humla, Mugu, Dolpa and Kalikot districts. According to Parmananda Acharya (personal communication), a campaigner for Jumli, it originated from the Sinja Valley of Jumla and extended to the Karnali region over the past 200 years.

7.3.1   *Personal Activities*

Figure 7.2 shows the use of Jumli language among Jumli mother tongue speakers in some of the main personal activities.

The figure shows that Jumli is widely used in joking, quarrelling and abusing. However, in the activities of singing outside, praying, counting, discussing, shopping/ marketing and village/ community meetings, Nepali is more widely used. In the activities of singing inside, praying and telling stories to others Jumli and Nepali are almost equal in use. Unlike the case of Dotyali, Hindi occupies no space in any of the personal activities mentioned above. And, English appears to be used to some extent in the activities of singing inside, counting, discussing, shopping/ marketing and telling stories to others.

7.3.2   *Formal Situations/Activities*

Table 7.5 shows language use by Jumli mother tongue speakers in formal situations/ activities.

The table indicates that Nepali is more dominant in all the activities mentioned in the table. Jumli, the local language of the community, is used in the course of reading and writing, talking to teachers and public activities/ceremonies to some extent, yet, it is less used than Nepali. The table also shows that English appears in many formal activities. However,

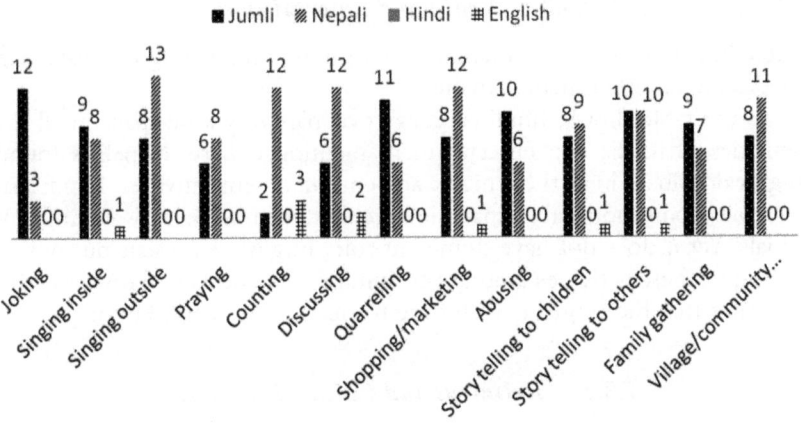

Fig. 7.2 Language use in personal activities. (Source: Thapa et al. 2018)

Table 7.5 Use of language in formal situations/activities (number of respondents)

Formal situations/ activities	Languages used by Jumli mother tongue speakers				
	Jumli	Nepali	Hindi	English	Others
Reading and writing	4	11	–	5	–
Seeking jobs	2	12	–	2	–
Sitting exams		13	–	7	–
Talking to teachers/professors	4	13	–	3	–
Talking to intellectuals	2	13	–	1	–
Offices and working places	1	13	–	2	–
Social/ political activities		13	–	–	–
Public activities and ceremonies	5	9	–	1	–
Administrative activities (document works)		13	–	3	–

Source: Thapa et al. (2018)

its use is not as widespread as Nepali. Hindi does not appear in any of the activities mentioned. The reason for the use of Nepali compared to Jumli is its use in most formal, official situations. As a typical remark by a Jumli respondent has it:

> *We go to Nepalgunj for jobs and education and bring back English and other languages to our community.* (Thapa et al. 2018)

7.3.3   Media and Entertainment

Table 7.6 shows the use of language by Jumli mother tongue speakers in media and entertainment activities.

As the table shows, Jumli language occupies very little space in all the activities of media and entertainment mentioned here. Nepali is found highly dominant in all these media and entertainment activities. Hindi also occupies some noticeable space in listening to music and watching TV serials. Yet it does not have dominant role. English is present but not so strong in these activities among the Jumli native speakers. However, this indicates that the language is shifting towards English and Hindi.

7.3.4   Religious and Cultural Activities

Table 7.7 shows the language use of language among Jumli mother tongue speakers in religious and cultural activities.

The Table shows that Jumli and Nepali are used equally in all these religious and cultural activities. Even so, except the case of marriage, Jumli is slightly more popular than Nepali. Other languages including Hindi and English have almost no presence in Jumli mother tongue speakers' religious and cultural activities.

7.3.5   Family and Friends

Table 7.8 illustrates language use by Jumli mother tongue speakers in the domain of family and friends.

Table 7.6 Use of language by Jumli mother tongue speakers in media and entertainment activities (number of respondents)

Media and entertainment activities	Languages used by Jumli mother tongue speakers				
	Jumli	Nepali	Hindi	English	Others
Watching TV serials	–	12	3	–	–
Watching TV news	1	13	1	–	–
Listening to music	2	11	6	–	–
Listening to news	1	13	–	1	–
Listening to and watching interviews	1	12	–	1	–
Reading newspapers	1	12	–	1	–
Reading horoscopes	1	11	–	1	–

Source: Thapa et al. (2018)

Table 7.7 Use of language in religious and cultural activities (number of respondents)

Religious and cultural activities	Languages used by Jumli mother tongue speakers				
	Jumli	Nepali	Hindi	English	Others
Religious festivals	8	5	–	–	–
Cultural programs (mass)	7	7	–	1	–
Death rites and rituals	8	6	–	–	–
Marriage	7	9	–	–	–
Birth rituals	7	6	–	–	–
Cultural festivals	9	6	–	–	–

Source: Thapa et al. (2018)

Table 7.8 Use of language with family and friends (number of respondents)

Family and friends	Languages used by Jumli mother tongue speakers				
	Jumli	Nepali	Hindi	English	Others
Father	10	7	–	–	–
Mother	10	6	–	–	–
Brothers/ sisters	9	8	–	–	–
Spouse	7	6	–	–	–
Friends at home	10	11	–	–	–
Friends outside	6	13	–	2	–

Source: Thapa et al. (2018)

The table shows that Jumli is more dominant in communicating with family and friends. Nepali occupies comparable space for communicating with family and friends at home. Jumli is more dominant in communicating with family members, whereas Nepali is more dominant in communicating with friends outside. Regarding the dominance of Jumli in the family at home and Nepali outside home, a Jumli woman (30) said,

> I use Jumli at home because it is connected to my identity, yet I have to use Nepali as I go outside, because Nepali is important to connect myself with the outside world. (Interview, April 2018)

This indicates that, in Jumla, Jumli is limited to communication within family and with friends.

7.4   Language Shift in Tharu

Tharu is one of the major Indo-Aryan languages of Nepal, spoken by 1,737,470 people (CBS 2011) in the Terai and inner Terai region of Nepal. It is spoken from Saptari district in the east of Nepal to Kailali and Kanchanpur districts in the west . Chitwaniya, Dangora and Rana are the major varieties of Tharu languages. Tharu people also speak and understand other neighboring languages such as Maithili, Bhojpuri and Awadhi, and Nepali, the official language of Nepal.

7.4.1   Personal Activities

Figure 7.3 demonstrates language use among the Tharu mother tongue speakers in the domain of personal activities

As the figure shows, in the activities of singing inside, quarreling, abusing and family gathering, Tharu language among its users. However, Tharu and Nepali are used more or less equally in joking, praying and shifting, a trend observed not only in practical use but also in linguistic aspects. There are many Nepali lexicons mixed in the Tharu language. The Tharu people of Dang concede that the popularity of Nepali is increasing among them. It is dominant in the activities of singing outside, shopping/ marketing, telling stories to others and village/ community meetings. Hindi has some influence among the Tharu speakers in the activities of

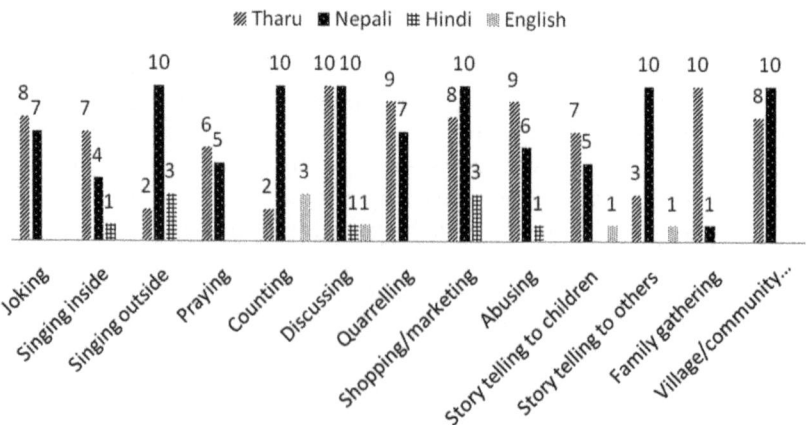

Fig. 7.3 Language use in personal activities. (Source: Thapa et al. 2018)

singing outside and shopping/ marketing. English appears in the case of counting, telling stories to children and verbal abusing, but its use is less widespread than Nepali and Tharu.

The analysis of both qualitative and quantitative data indicates that Nepali is more dominant and used widely among Tharu mother tongue speakers. The language is easy to understand and there are many benefits of learning it. A man involved in the hotel business remarked,

> *Haami ta sabai bhasa bolcham ra bujcham pani. Yo pesama bhasa jane pachi nikkai sajilo hune rahecha. aile nepali ta sabaile bujchchan ra bolchhan pani"*
> [We speak all languages; If a person is familiar with all languages, then it is easy to carry on this profession. Nowadays all people understand and speak Nepali]. (Interview, April 2018)

As the field study was conducted in semi-urban locations (where people of different mother tongues communicate with Nepali), the influence of Nepali among Tharu speakers was particularly marked.

7.4.2   Formal Situations/ Activities

Table 7.9 shows the use of language among Tharu mother tongue speakers in the domain of formal situations/ activities.

Table 7.9 Use of language in formal situations and activities (number of respondents)

Formal situations/ activities	Languages used by Tharu mother tongue speakers			
	Tharu	Nepali	Hindi	English
Reading and writing	–	10	–	2
Seeking jobs	–	9	1	4
Sitting exams	1	8	–	4
Talking to teachers/ professors	1	10	–	3
Talking to intellectuals	1	10	1	4
Offices and working places	–	10	–	2
Social/ political activities	3	10	–	–
Public activities and ceremonies	5	10	1	–
Administrative activities (document works)	–	10	–	–

Source: Thapa et al. (2018)

In the case of Tharu mother tongue speakers, Nepali is highly dominant in most formal situations. Tharu does occupy a little space in the activities of sitting exams, talking to teachers and intellectuals, social/political and public activities; however, it is not so strongly used as Nepali. English has a clearly visible presence among these people; it has significant presence in reading and writing, sitting exams, talking to teachers, talking to intellectuals and in offices and workplaces.

7.4.3   Media and Entertainment

Table 7.10 depicts the language use by Tharu mother tongue speakers particularly focusing on the activities of media and entertainment.

As presented in the table, Tharu speakers use the Nepali language while engaging in media and entertainment activities. As the data indicate, in the activities of watching TV serials, watching TV news, listening to music, listening to/ watching interviews, reading newspapers and reading horoscopes, Nepali is widely used. Hindi occupies more space in watching TV serials and listening to music. English is also present to some extent in media and entertainment activities; but it is less dominant than Hindi. The presence of Tharu is notable particularly in listening to music, though less dominant than Nepali and Hindi.

7.4.4   Religious and Cultural Activities

Table 7.11 demonstrates the use of language among Tharu mother tongue speakers in religious and cultural activities.

Table 7.10   Use of language in media and entertainment (number of respondents)

Media and entertainment activities	Languages used by Tharu mother tongue speakers				
	Tharu	Maithili	Nepali	Hindi	English
Watching TV serials	1	–	8	9	1
Watching TV news		–	10	1	2
Listening to music	4	–	8	9	–
Listening to news	1	1	10	2	1
Listening to & watching interviews	1	–	10	2	1
Reading newspapers	–	–	10		3
Reading horoscopes	–	–	10	–	–1

Source: Thapa et al. (2018)

Table 7.11 Use of language in religious and cultural activities (number of respondents)

Religious/ cultural activities	Languages used by Tharu mother tongue speakers				
	Tharu	Nepali	Hindi	English	Others
Religious festivals	10	2			
Cultural programs (mass)	10	5			
Death rites and rituals	10	2			
Marriage ceremonies	9	6	1		
Birth rituals	10	4			
Cultural festivals	8	7	2		

Source: Thapa et al. (2018)

Table 7.12 Use of language with family and friends (number of respondents)

Family and friends	Tharu	Nepali	Hindi	English	Others
Father	10	2	–	–	–
Mother	10	3	–	–	–
Brothers/ sisters	10	6	–	–	–
Spouse	6	3	–	–	–
Friends at home	10	9	–	–	–
Friends outside	3	10	–	–	–

Source: Thapa et al. (2018)

The table indicates that the Tharu language is very dominant in religious and cultural activities but that presence of Nepali is noticeable in all sorts of religious–cultural activities covered in the study. Similar levels of use of the two languages occur in cultural festivals. Overall, Nepali is not dominant over Tharu.

7.4.5 Family and Friends

Table 7.12 displays the languages used by Tharu mother tongue speakers while communicating with family and friends.

As in the case of religious and cultural activities, Tharu is dominantly used in communication with parents, siblings, spouse and friends at home. However, Nepali is found in use in each of the cases covered in the study. While communicating with friends outside home, Nepali is highly dominant. However, no presence of Hindi and English was seen in the data.

7.5   Language Shift in Nepali

Nepali is the official language of Nepal. It is spoken by more than 16 million people in Nepal as their mother tongue and understood by almost all the people of Nepal. Nepali is also spoken in India, Bhutan, Burma and many other countries by Nepali people. The Nepali language has many geographical and social varieties. Nepali has a rich heritage of oral literature as well as a body of written literature that has been developed during last two and half centuries. The vocabulary and writing system has been influenced by and developed from Sanskrit and recorded with the Devanagari script. Modern Nepali has borrowed vocabulary from Sanskrit, English and Hindi languages. This section is concerned with the exploration of shifting from Nepali to other language/s in the various domains covered by the study.

7.5.1   Personal Activities

From the data projected in the diagram given below, we can see the trend of language use among Nepali native speakers (Fig. 7.4).

Clearly, Nepali has been used more dominantly by Nepali mother tongue speakers in all the personal activities. Occurrence of Hindi and English is also seen in the personal activities of Nepali speakers but none

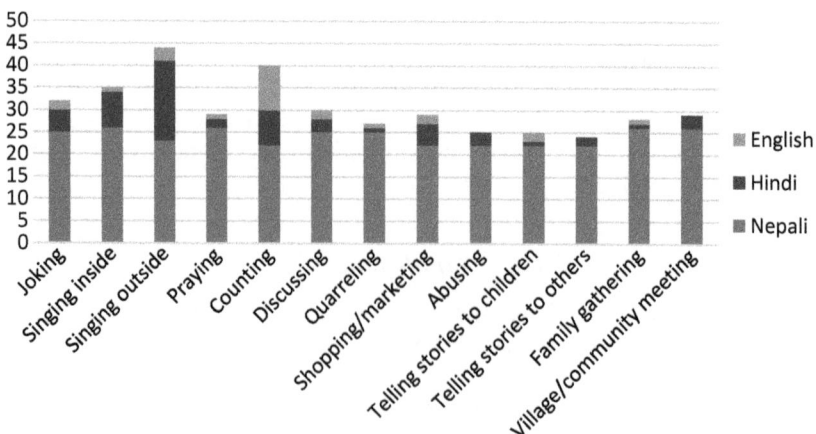

Fig. 7.4 Language use in personal activities. (Source: Thapa et al. 2018)

of these languages has dominated Nepali in any personal activity. The presence of Hindi is considerable in the activities of singing (inside and outside). In the same way, English is in use by these speakers to a considerable extent in counting and to some extent in discussing.

7.5.2 Formal Situation/ Activities

Table 7.13 indicates the trend of language use among Nepali native speakers in formal situations and activities.

Among Nepali mother tongue speakers, as depicted in the table, a strong tendency of using Nepali is found in all the activities mentioned here. However, the use of English is clearly noticeable in the activities of reading/ writing, seeking jobs, sitting exams, talking to teachers and using language for official purpose. But its use is distinctly less than the use of Nepali. The presence of Bhojpuri and Maithili is noticeable to a small extent in these speakers, but it is limited to the areas where these languages are spoken in the local community such as Dhanusha, Saptari and Parsa districts.

7.5.3 Media and Entertainment

Table 7.14 demonstrates the languages used by Nepali mother tongue speakers in media and entertainment activities.

Table 7.13 Use of language in formal situations/ activities (number of respondents)

Formal situations/activities	Languages used by Nepali mother tongue speakers					
	Sanskrit	Bhojpuri	Maithili	Nepali	Hindi	English
Reading and writing	–	–	1	27	–	11
Seeking jobs	–	–	1	24	1	11
Sitting exams	1	–	–	27	–	15
Talking to teachers/ professors	–	1	–	24	1	13
Talking to intellectuals	–	–	–	27	1	6
Offices and working places	–	1		24	1	11
Social/ political activities	–	2	2	28	1	3
Public activities and ceremonies	–	2	2	28	3	3
Administrative activities (document works)	–	2	–	27	–	5

Source: Thapa et al. (2018)

Table 7.14   Use of language in media and entertainment (number of respondents)

Media and entertainment activities	Languages used by Nepali mother tongue speakers					
	Maithili	Bhojpuri	Tamang	Nepali	Hindi	English
Watching TV serials	–	1	1	25	20	11
Watching TV news	–	–	–	28	9	10
Listening to music	1	1	1	27	20	11
Listening to news	1	1	1	25	8	8
Listening to and watching interviews	1	1	–	27	7	7
Reading newspapers	–	1	–	26	6	11
Reading horoscopes	–	1	–	25	4	6

Source: Thapa et al. (2018)

Nepali is dominant in all the activities of media and entertainment as mentioned in the table, followed by Hindi and English. The presence of Hindi is stronger than English for listening to music and watching TV serials, while in the case of watching TV or radio news and interviews the occurrence of these two languages looks similar. The presence of Bhojpuri is also noticeable in the Bhojpuri-speaking locality to a small extent. Maithili and Tamang are also found in use but limited to fewer activities.

7.5.4   Religious and Cultural Activities

The use of different languages among Nepali mother tongue speakers for religious and cultural purpose is depicted in Table 7.15.

Clearly, Nepali is used more than any other language in all the religious and cultural activities/ We can see the presence of Sanskrit, Maithili, Bhojpuri, Hindi and English languages but they are not as dominant as Nepali. This indicates that Nepali is not being affected very much by language shifting towards other languages.

7.5.5   Family and Friends

The use of languages by Nepali mother tongue speakers in communication with the family members and friends is depicted in Table 7.16.

As the table demonstrates, Nepali dominates in communicating with the family members as well as friends at home. In the same way, all the

Table 7.15 Use of language in religious and cultural activities (number of respondents)

Religious and cultural activities	Languages used by Nepali mother tongue speakers					
	Sanskrit	Maithili	Bhojpuri	Nepali	Hindi	English
Religious festivals	1	1	1	28	1	–
Cultural programs (mass)	–	1	2	26	4	1
Death rites and rituals	–	2	2	27	1	1
Marriage ceremonies	–	2	3	26	–	–
Birth rituals	1	3	1	26	â	–
Cultural festivals	–	2	1	27	2	1

Source: Thapa et al. (2018)

Table 7.16 Use of language with family and friends (number of respondents)

Family and friends	Languages used by Nepali mother tongue speakers						
	Tamang	Bhojpuri	Maithili	Nepali	Hindi	English	Others
Father	–	–	1	27	–	3	–
Mother	–	–	1	28	–	2	–
Brother/ sister	–	–	1	28	–	6	–
Spouse	–	–		22	–	3	–
Friends at home	–	3	1	28	1	3	–
Friends outside	1	3	1	28	4	6	–

Source: Thapa et al. (2018)

speakers were found using Nepali while communicating with friends outside home. Interestingly, English is used, though to a small extent, in communication within the family as well as with friends outside, though its use is not comparable with Nepali. Presence of Bhojpuri, Maithili and Hindi is noticeable among Nepali mother tongue speakers in some cases (though small in extent), but such instances are confined to specific areas.

7.6   Intergenerational Shift

A significant concern in the study of language shift is the change in reasons people choose to use one or other language/s from one generation to the next. In this regard, it would be relevant to see whether (and how far) the speakers of a new generation are adopting their mother tongue or using another/ additional language/s. Regarding the pattern of intergenerational shift of this kind, though all the domains of language use are not analyzed in this brief study, the domain of personal activities is considered for a brief analysis.

Some indications of language shift can be noted in a couple of personal activities. For instance, use of Jumli mother tongue is not found in the age group of 15–25 years in the activity of murmuring, though the speakers of older generations are found using Jumli for the same activity.

More interesting here is the case of language use in the activity of counting applicable in Dotyali, Jumli, and Tharu. In this regard, absence of the use of Dotyali as well as Jumli is noticed in the age group of 15–25, though it is present in older generations. Likewise, speakers of Tharu language in this age group are not found using their mother tongue in counting, while the older generations do use the mother tongue for this purpose. As revealed from personal interviews, members of Tharu and Dotyali language community in the age group of 15–25 hardly use native words for daily activities and cultural activities. However, older generations very commonly use various words and expressions in their daily communication.

Most of the adults in the Tharu community interviewed during the fieldwork said that they used Tharu while talking to their older generations, but Nepali when communicating with the younger ones. Such a shift has been found among younger generation towards Nepali and even English (to some extent), reinforced by the growing influence of modern media and technology. The generation gap among the different age groups is illustrated in a remark made by a Dotyali man (56) who said,

> *I myself and my wife like to listen Dotyali songs in radio and TV programs, but my daughter prefers Hindi serials, she always watches these serials, and our son enjoys sports mostly in English language.* (Interview, February 2018)

Similar cases can be observed in the Jumli language community. The members of the older generation often use Jumli language whereas it is less used by the members of younger generations. For example, a Jumli man (62), while talking about intergenerational language shift, said,

> *ke garnu sir, haami ta bolcham ni tara aaileka ketaketiharu bolnai mandainan; ajjha boarding padneharu ta Englishma bolchan"* [What to do, we speak Jumli but our children do not want to speak this language, even those who go to boarding school speak English instead of Jumli]. (Interview, April 2018)

This is evidenced in the quantitative analysis of some minority languages as well. For example, in the activities of telling stories to children as well as others, use of Dotyali and Tharu was absent in the age group of 15–25 years—even though the older generations are still using these languages for the same purpose. In the case of Tharu mother tongue speakers, storytelling in Tharu language was confined to people of 60+.

However, in the case of Nepali and Tharu languages, younger generation people (15–25 years) were found using the mother tongue in all the personal activities covered by this study. Tharu speakers used their native tongue in the domains of cultural, religious and some formal situations as well. And in the case of Nepali-language speakers, they used it in both of the domains. However, the data indicates that the young generation of mother tongue speakers (including the speakers of Nepali) are being gradually motivated to other "dominant" languages under the influence of globalization, education, migration, business and communication, and technologies and the media.

7.7   Summary

Overall, cases of language shift signify that the use of mother tongues (other than Nepali) is found more in the family and cultural or religious activities. However, such mother tongues are not dominantly used for communication in outside domains and contact areas such as marketplaces and business activities. Importantly, the use of the mother tongue (again, other than Nepali) is less in formal activities including education and administration. In the case of immediate community or surroundings, the tendency to use the mother tongue as well as a second language is found to be applicable in more or less all languages. The shift of languages from one another in a multilingual country like Nepal is really complex, and has created many obstacles in developing an appropriate language policy for the nation. People use language according to their needs and interests, which symbolizes civilization. The existence of multilingualism in a state, regardless of its origins, implies a hierarchy among languages (Far and Song 2011: 658). So, the high degree of shifting of minority languages towards Nepali, English and Hindi is an indication of developing monolingual ideology in the future. Considering the trend across generations, however, indications of the reduced use of mother tongues (except for Nepali) is noticeable among new generations, a process which is affected by media, education and globalization. Nonetheless, older generations are maintaining the use of their mother tongue in several ways.

BIBLIOGRAPHY

Central Bureau of Statistics. (2011). *Population of Nepal.* Kathmandu: National Planning Commission.

Far, M., & Song, J. (2011). Language ideologies and policies: Multilingualism and Education. *Language and linguistics Compass, 5*(9), 650–665.

Thapa, R., Luitel, B., Gautam, B. L., & Devkota, K. R. (2018). *Language shift in Nepal: A general study.* A report submitted to Language Commission Nepal, Kathmandu.

CHAPTER 8

Language Contact and Implications to Language Policies

8.1　Introduction

The discussions in the previous sections have pointed out the linguistic geography of Nepal, and history, census and policy provisions regarding the status and use of languages in Nepal. Various patterns, causes, and impacts on language contact and shift from various ideological perspectives have been interpreted in the context of Nepal. Emphasis has been given to concern on the way ideology enters into face-to face speaking practice to create an interactional space in which the subconscious and automatic sociolinguistic processes of interpretation and inference can generate a variety of outcomes (Gumperz 1982: 3). The trends of language contact have been explored with reference to diverse activities under different domains of language use and attitudes among Sherpa-, Newar- and Maithili-speaking communities (See Chaps. 3, 4 and 5) along with a general trend of language shift in Nepal (Chap. 6). The causes and impacts of language contact and shift are further explored and discussed in the light of personal anecdotes, narratives and stories from the field. The analysis of both quantitative and qualitative generated the following findings.

8.2   TRENDS OF LANGUAGE CONTACT IN NEPAL

The research studies in this book demonstrate that mother tongues are strongly used in personal activities in informal settings within the family and language community. While exploring the language used by Sherpa, Newar, Tharu, Limbu, Jumli, Dotyali and Maithili, it has been found that these languages are spoken within families and immediate communities. However, the speakers of these languages shift to Nepali language when they interact with interlingual social groups.

In most of the cases of languages within Kathmandu Valley and outside, mother tongues are used noticeably in the activities of joking, singing inside, quarrelling, family gathering, telling stories to the children, and religious and ritual activities of the respective language groups. However, Nepali is used more in activities such as counting, shopping/ marketing, community meetings, singing outside, telling stories to others and cultural programs.

In the formal activities such as reading and writing, seeking jobs, sitting exams, talking to teachers and intellectuals, communicating in offices and workplaces, social/ political activities and administrative works, the Nepali language has been observed to be dominant over mother tongues.

In the activities of watching TV serials, watching TV news, listening to music, listening to and watching interviews, reading newspapers and reading horoscopes mentioned in the domain of media and entertainment, the Nepali language has been found to be extensively used compared to the mother tongues like Sherpa, Newar, Tharu and Maithili. In these activities, a shifting pattern from the mother tongues to Nepali, and even to Hindi and English have been observed remarkably consistently.

In the domain of family and friends, both mother tongues and Nepali languages are commonly in use. However, mother tongues have been found in wide use in the activities of communicating with father, mother, siblings, spouse and friends at home. In contrast, the Nepali language has been more widely used while communicating with friends outside home environment.

Nepali language has been in a dominant position among the mother tongue use in all domains of activities in Sherpa, Newar and Maithili communities. However, there is a noticeable influence of Hindi in the activities of listening and watching TV serials under the media and entertainment domain. Likewise, it has also been observed that there is an increasing influence of English in formal situations/ activities. This sort of influence indicates the complex shifting patterns of language in people's daily communication. Among the three generations in terms of age groups, so far studied (15–25 yrs., 25–55 yrs. and 55+ yrs.), younger generations are less motivated to use their mother tongues. They are found picking up limited lexicons and simple chunks/patterns of their mother tongues rather than acquiring their mother tongues in a full-fledged manner.

The trend of language shift in Nepal is home language toward official Nepali language and then to English in all aspects of society. So the government and concerned agencies should think carefully about how to preserve the languages and cultural heritage of Nepal.

8.3   Causes and Impacts of Language Contact in Nepal

The information obtained from the interview and questionnaire reveals that the media, migration and marriage (M3) have played influential roles and become major causes of language contact and shift. Market forces and the consequent economic benefits are the major determinants of that. In a similar vein, the state's political–ideological intervention in diverse social aspects including schooling/ education is found to have a strong effect in reinforcing language shift, that is the shift from local mother tongues to dominant national, regional and global languages. People's motivation and migration for economic benefit have also been noted as keys to encouraging people to adopt languages that deploy more instrumental functions in their job market.

Various attitudinal impacts preserve mother tongue as the language of ethnolinguistic identity and communal solidarity. The speakers of mother tongues studied in this research have associated their languages with their ethnic identity, and Nepali (and also English) with more pragmatic/ instrumental functions.

Motivational impact retains Nepali and also some dominant regional and global languages as the language of interlingual communication, and that of fulfilling and achieving instrumental needs. Globalized market forces have been found key drivers motivating people belonging to diverse mother tongues towards Nepali, and even to English and other languages spoken where Nepali people migrate to access of education, jobs, business success, and so on. These opinions project the vivid nature and forms of language contact and shifts. The causes and impacts are mainly attitudinal and motivational, may be due to diverse social environments and co-existing ideologies. Perhaps the most important characteristic of the social environments in which we live is their unprecedented cultural and ethnic diversity (Gumperz 1982: 2). It can be observed how the social and political condition of modern life favors the creation of new linguistic symbols which can serve as the gathering point for interest group sharing. In this regard, the multilingualism of Nepal has created and developed a unique environment in language contact study from different ideological perspectives.

8.4   IMPLICATIONS OF RESEARCH FOR LANGUAGE POLICY

There are many implications for language policy in research of this nature, whether based on language contact studies in the context of Kathmandu Valley or outside Nepal. This comprehensive study has opened many avenues for devising more practical language policies, future research and collaborations in many micro and macro areas of sociolinguistic studies.

8.4.1   Policy-Level Implications

Language contact and shift may lead to decline and death of local mother tongues. Thus, such shifts need to be intervened against by the state in order to preserve them. The state should conduct extensive situation analysis (by survey study) to assess the current status of Nepali languages and their shifting trends into Nepali, even to English and Hindi and other regional and global languages. Bilingual and multilingual language policies may work well to preserve and promote local mother tongues even in the event of increasing language contact and shift.

Language revitalization programs are almost essential to implement at the level of local, provincial and federal governments. Concerned stakeholders and language agencies should promote mother tongue revitalization programs. In order to do so, local mother tongues need to be incorporated in the framework of multilingual education, mother tongue education and inclusive education that have been emphasized by the Constitution of Nepal (2015).

Many speakers of local languages are not aware on the value of their own language in preserving ethnic and cultural identities. They might be guided by the use of official, second and foreign languages and the most powerful international languages ideologies. Hence, there is a need to bring change in the mindset of local language users by promoting mother-tongue based multilingual language education policies from the beginning of their schooling.

As media has been identified as one of the major causes of language contact and shift, different programs can be developed and broadcast so as to develop awareness on language-related issues. The language ideology of individual users is a complex notion to generalize and often dynamic. It implies that different ideologies dealing with the issue of language use have been developed over time. So, the information on those ideologies and their critiques can be made visible by means of different language-related publications.

In practice, virtually all participants draw on different ideologies at different times, sometimes referring to perceived problems relating to multilingualism, at other times to perceived benefits. This variability within individuals is a noted feature of language ideologies. Kroskrity (2000) attributes it to the multiplicity of meaningful social divisions (class, gender, clan, elites, generations etc.) within sociocultural groups that have the potential to produce different perspectives expressed as keys of group membership (p. 12). In all cases, however, participants seem to creatively select whatever they "need" from available language ideologies to best represent their own interests in multilingual Nepal and its unique setting. So the language ideology of Sherpa differs from Newar, Maithili, Tharu and others. Sherpa living in Kathmandu have been influenced by economic activity rather than ethnic or linguistic solidarity. Newar, Maithili and Tharu have been affected by globalization, media, education and communication with much intergenerational shift.

8.4.2   Research-Level Implications

Language contact is a natural linguistic phenomenon in multilingual countries like Nepal. This phenomenon needs to be studied more extensively in its social and historical context where multiple languages are in contact and influence one another over a long time. The patterns of language shift vary from one language to another, one geographical location to another, one social situation to another. Thus, study needs to be specific in terms of language and space. Only then, there could be more exploration in depth and range of language contact and shift in a multilingual country like Nepal.

Language contact and shift is a collective process. It may be observed not only in instrumental functions of language use but also at the pho-netic/ phonemic level, the lexical level, the grammatical level and the semantic level. Linguistic study of these aspects in language-contact situa-tions needs to be launched extensively. The trends and patterns of lan-guage contact and shift differ in terms of age groups, gender and literacy level. Thus, cross-generational patterns of language contact and shift need to be explored, focusing on specific mother tongues.

The effects of language contact and shift need to be explored further so as to see the interconnection of diverse social aspects such as education, marriage, migration, business, media consumption and language-shift pat-terns. Studies need to be carried out on how these causes reinforce lan-guage contact, especially from less-dominant languages and mother tongues to more dominant languages.

This study on the language contact situation in Sherpa, Newar, Tharu, Jumli, Dotyali and Maithili communities has explored different patterns of language contact. There is still a need for more qualitative studies of the similar issue of other ethnic and minority languages of Nepal. In such cases, this study can be helpful for both theoretical and methodological insights for further researches and studies.

8.5   RECOMMENDATIONS FOR LANGUAGE POLICY AND PLANNING

Countries like Nepal, where majority languages are endangered, should be emphasizing language policy. Small and minority languages need extra care and preservation. A free-language economy will result in the extinc-tion of many ethnic and minority languages. In this context, language planning is necessary to stop the liberal policy of language economy where language is compared with benefits and commodity markets. The compre-hensive research on Sherpa community living in Kathmandu valley shows that Sherpa do not speak and maintain their heritage language because of tourism, employment and many other reasons (Gautam 2020). So we need to develop language attitude criteria or surveys in order to assess the situation of language contact and shift. Language shift occurs through deliberate decisions that directly or indirectly affect languages and reflects economic, political, cultural, social and technological changes. It is. there-fore, possible to analyze and determine what causes language shift. Social and political factors, and not just evolution, are at work in language loss and decay. Politics and power, prejudice and discrimination are some of the causes of language decline and death.

Language planning and policy in Nepal has not yet been systematized or taken seriously by the government. Ethnolinguistic heterogeneity was not officially recognized in Nepalese official policy until 1990 (Pradhan 2018: 2). The establishment of multiparty democracy brought some significant changes in policy. Some important work has already been started by individuals and institutions with the support of various funding agencies. The linguistic survey of Nepal (2008–2018) has undertaken a sociolinguistic survey of about 86 different languages (Gautam 2019). The Central Department of Linguistics, Tribhuvan University has developed documentation (basic grammar and lexicon) of about 30 languages with the support of various national and international institutions and agencies. Likewise, the language commission of Nepal, which was established in 2016, has done some preliminary work (survey, documentation and description) on some minority and endangered languages. So the collection and evaluation of all the previous works on Nepalese languages should be collected, analyzed and evaluated. In order to find out the real picture and profile of Nepalese languages, the government of Nepal should conduct a separate linguistic census. This can be done with the help of provincial and local governmental bodies which can generate an accurate picture of Nepalese languages. After making a clear profile of Nepalese languages we can adopt the following three established models of language planning through careful management system.

8.5.1 Corpus Planning

More than 80% of Nepal's languages lack standardization of grammar and writing system, modernized terminologies, sufficient vocabularies and the description of other features. So the preservation and development of basic parts of all ethnic and minority languages is very important. Some work has been going on but it should be systematized and handled carefully. At least a basic corpus planning should be begun on the major languages spoken in the country immediately before they lose their mother tongue speakers and move towards majority languages. It is necessary to document and describe the basic features of many languages like Kumal, Bote, Jumli, Kaike, Lungkhim, Lohwa, Dhuleli, Thulung, Bajjika, Danuwar, Lohrung and so on. This is necessary to prepare literacy materials and primers for education in mother tongues.

8.5.2   Status Planning

Regarding the official status of Nepal's languages, the Constitution of Nepal (2015) has clearly defined the recognition and status of languages. Status planning is attempting politically to gain more recognition, functions and capacity for the languages spoken in Nepal. By maintaining the use of language in family domains and sometimes spreading into new language domains, a language may hopefully be secured and revitalized. After the implementation of the 2015 Constitution and the practice of federalism in Nepal, languages need to be encouraged towards status planning when they will have legal and official status at local and provincial levels. The use of these languages needs to be increased in media, education, law and administration. The establishment of a language commission (2016) is also a progressive step towards status planning for Nepal's languages. It will establish and recognize some more languages like Dotyali in Karnali province, Maithili and Bhojpuri in Province Two, Tamang and Newar in Bagmati province, Gurung and Magar in Gandaki province, Limbu and other languages in Province One and so on. However, speakers of small and minority languages may be influenced by such change in status planning. So the opportunity planning for daily use of the minority languages is essential (Baker 2006: 51).

8.5.3   Acquisition Planning

Acquisition planning is necessary for creating various domains of language use in teaching and learning activities in schools, adult learning classes, and literacy programs and so on. It is particularly concerned with language reproduction in the family and school through a revitalization campaign. In many minority languages of Nepal, there are families who use Nepali or other dominant neighboring languages with their children. This trend is increasing among most of the ethnic and minority languages because parents believe that there are economic, employment or educational advantages in speaking a majority languages e.g. Nepali, English, Hindi to the children. A lack of family language reproduction is a major and direct cause of language shift (Baker 2006: 52) so that we can develop a unique language-acquisition planning in order to encourage parents who speak minority languages to raise their children bilingually and revitalize languages in community cultural activities and sometimes in schools through mother tongue based education.

The government of Nepal should start immediately, with the help of language planners, policy makers, sociologists, anthropologists, economists and development specialists, to formulate a better language policy for the country.

8.6 Summary

This chapter summarizes the findings and information collected in this book and tries to see some possibilities of language contact studies in the future for research and policy level recommendations. Language revitalization programs are essential to implement at the level of local, provincial and federal governments. The concerned stakeholders and language agencies should promote the use of mother tongue revitalization programs. The trends and patterns of language contact and shift differ in terms of age groups, gender and literacy level. Thus, cross-generational patterns of language contact and shift need to be explored, focusing on the specific mother tongues. Language planning and policy in Nepal has not yet been systematized or taken seriously by the government. The government and concerned stakeholders can adopt the three common models of language planning (Status, Corpus and Acquisition) through a careful management system.

Bibliography

Baker, C. (2006). *Foundations of bilingual education and bilingualism* (4th ed.). Clevedon, UK: Multilingual Matters.

Gautam, B. L. (2019). Sociolinguistic survey of Nepalese languages: A critical evaluation. *Language Ecology, 3*(2), 190–208. John Benjamin's Publishing Company.

Gautam, B. L. (2020). *Language contact in Kathmandu.* An unpublished PhD dissertation, Tribhuvan University, Kathmandu.

Government of Nepal. (2015). *The constitution of Nepal 2015.* Kathmandu: Minister of Law and Justice.

Gumperz, J. J. (1982). *Language and social identity.* Cambridge, UK: Cambridge University Press.

Kroskrity, P. V. (2000). Regimenting languages: Language ideological perspectives. In P. V. Kroskrity (Ed.), *Regimes of language: Ideologies, polities, and identities.* Santa Fe, NM: School of American Research Press.

Pradhan, U. (2018). Simultaneous identities: Ethnicity and nationalism in mother tongue education in Nepal. In *Nations and Nationalism* (pp. 1–21). ASEN/John Wiley& Sons Ltd.

Sociolinguistic Questionnaire: Language Use and Language Attitude in the Nepalese Context

META DATA (BASELINE INFORMATION)

Question	Answer
1. Interview Number	
2. Date	
3. Place of Interview	
4. Interpreter Name (if needed)	

5. Name of the informant: ....

    (a) □ Male   (b) □ Female   (c) □ Other ....

6. Age group: (i) □ 5-19   (ii) □ 20-40   (iii) 40-60   (iii) □ 60+

7. What is your educational background?

    (a) Illiterate   (b) Informal   (c) Formal

8. (If "Formal") What year/level did you complete?

    (a) Primary   (b) Lower Secondary   (c) Secondary

    (d) Higher (specify highest degree) ....

8. Your Profession/Job.......................

10. Marital status: (a) Married   (b) Single   (c) Divorced

11. (If "Married") Do you have any children?

    (a) Yes   (b) No

12. Caste & Ethnic group: ....

13. What is your mother tongue?..............

14. Your mother's mother tongue............

15. Your father's mother tongue...............

16. Mother tongue of your husband/ wife ....

17. Where were you born ?

(a) Ward No......... (b)Village/Town.............   (c)VDC/municipality.............   (d)

District..............   (d) Zone..................

18. Where do you live now? ....

19. How many years have you been living here? ....

20. What are the reasons for/of living here? ....

21. Have you lived anywhere else for more than a year? ....

22. (if so) Where? When? How long did you live there? ....

23.Do you speak Nepali?

24.(If yes) Where did you learn to speak Nepali?

(a) Family   (b) Neighbor   (c) School   (c) Workplace

25.Do you speak English/Hindi ?

26.(If yes) How did you learn to speak English/Hindi?

(a) Family   (b) Neighbour   (c) School   (d) Workplace

27. What are the other languages do you speak?

(a).........(b)...........(c).........(d).............

LANGUAGE USE

28. Which language you think to be useful for the following activities? **(Social Activities)**

Activities/Languages	MT	Nepali	English	Hindi	others
Making friends					
Shopping					
Making telephone calls					
Talking with workers					
Talking with teachers/professors					
Talking with acdemicians					
Getting a job					
Reading and writing Passing Exams					

29. Which Languages do you speak with your relatives and friends? **(Family & Relations)**

Persons	Languages						
	Always MT	In MT more often Nepali	In Nepali more often MT	Always in Nepali	In Nepali and English	In Nepali and Hindi	Others

Father							
Mother							
Brother/sister							
Spouse							
Friends at home							
Friends in office/school/college							
Neighbours at home							
Neighbours outside							

30. Which language do you use very often in the following situations? (**Culture & religion**)

Situations	MT	Nepali	English	Hindi	Others
Religious Festivals					
Cultural programs					
Death ceremonies					
Marriage ceremonies					
Birth ceremonies					
Cultural festivals					

31. Which language do you use very often in the following situations? (**Official & Ceremonial**)

Situations	MT	Nepali	English	Hindi	Others
Office/work place					

Political/social gathering					
Public activities/fun fair					
Administration					
Strangers					

32. In which language do you experience or do the following? **(Media related activities)**

Activities/languages	Mother Tongue	Nepali	English	Hindi	Others
Watching movie/serial					
Watching news					
Listening music					
Listening Radio					
Listening interview					
Reading Newspaper					

LANGUAGE ATTITUDE

33. Which language do you use most frequently for the following purposes?

	Domains	Language
A	joking	

B	counting	
C	quarreling	
D	Singing inside	
E	Bargaining/shopping/marketing	
F	Abusing(scolding/using taboo)	
G	Praying	
H	Singing outside	
I	Discussing/Debate	
J	Family gathering	
K	Telling stories to children	
L	Telling stories to others	
M	Village/community meetings	
N		

34. How often do you use your mother tongue?

  (a) Every day   (b) Sometimes   (c) Rarely   (d)Never

35. How do you feel when you speak your MT?

  (a) Proud   (b) Embarrassed   (c) Neutral

36. When you speak your MT in the presence of the speaker of the dominant language what do you feel...

  (a) Prestigious   (b) Embarrassed   (c) Neutral

37. Have you ever had any problem because of being a native speaker of your mother tongue?

  (a) Yes   (b) No

38. (If "Yes") What kinds of problems have you had?

  (a) Social discrimination.

(a) Social discrimination.

(b) Political discrimination.

(c) Economic discrimination.

(d) Hostile confrontation.

(e) Discrimination in education.

(f) Social pressure.

(g) Political pressure.

(h) Economic pressure.

(i) Other

39. If there are two people come to work at your place having same skill and experiences, one speaks MT and another speaks Nepali, whom would you choose ?

A) MT   B) Nepali   C) Either   D) None

40. How often do you speak Nepali?

(a) Every day   (b) Sometimes   (c) Rarely   (d) Never

41. Why doyou like to use Nepali?

a. Easy   b. Prestigeous   c. Everybody likes   d. Just so/don't know

42. Why do you like to use English/Hindi?

a. Easy   b. Prestigeous   c. Everybody likes   d. Just so/don't know

43. Which language do you like to use most and why?

....

....

BIBLIOGRAPHY

Abbi, A. (1996). Languages of tribal & indigenous people of India. In *Languages in contact in Jharkhand* (pp. 131–147). New Delhi: Motilal Banarasidas Publishers.

Agnihotri, R. K. (2017). Identity and multilinguality: The case of India. In *Language policy, culture, and identity in Asian contexts* (pp. 185–204). London: Routledge. https://doi.org/10.4324/978135092034.

Aronin, L., & Singleton, D. (2008). Multilingualism as a new linguistic dispensation. *International Journal of Multilingualism, 5*(1), 1–16.

Atkinson, J., & Feather, N. (1966). *A theory of achievement motivation.* Volume 6: John Wiley & Sons, Inc.

Baker, C. (1992). *Attitudes and language.* Clevedon, UK: Multilingual Matters.

Baker, C. (2007). Becoming bilingual through bilingual education. In P. Auer & L. Wei (Eds.), *Handbook of multilingualism and multilingual communication* (pp. 131–152). Berlin: Mouton de Gruyter.

Bandhu, C. M. (1989). The role of national language in establishing the national unity. *Kailash, 15*, 121–134.

Bendix, H. E. (1974). Indo Aryan and Tibeto-Burman contact: As seen through Newari and Nepali verb tenses. *International Journal of Dravidian Linguistics,* III(I), India.

Bhattarai, G. B. (2006). English teaching situation in Nepal: Elaboration of The theme for panel discussion in the 40th TESOL conference. *Journal of NELTA, 11*, 17–23.

Blommaert, J. (2005). *Discourse: A critical introduction.* Cambridge, UK: Cambridge University Press.

© The Author(s), under exclusive license to Springer Nature   167
Switzerland AG 2021
B. L. Gautam, *Language Contact in Nepal,*
https://doi.org/10.1007/978-3-030-68810-3

Blommaert, J. (2010). *The sociolinguistics of globalization*. Cambridge and New York: Cambridge University Press.

Blommaert, J. (2013). Policy, policing, and the ecology of social norms: Ethnographic monitoring revisited. *International Journal of the Sociology of Language, 219*, 123–140.

Bloor, M., & Wood, F. (2006). *Key words in qualitative methods: A vocabulary of research concepts*. Thousand oaks, CA: Sage Publications Ltd..

Bourdieu, P. (1991). *Language and symbolic power*. Cambridge: Polity Press.

Brinkhaus, H. (1987). *Pradyumnavijaya-nataka* (of jagatprakashamalla). In *The Pradyumna-Prabhavati legend in Nepal: A study of the Hindu myth of the draining of the Nepal valley* (pp. 161–345). Stuttgart: Franz Steiner, Wiesbaden.

Brower, B. (1991). *Sherpa of Khumbu: People, livestock and landscape*. Delhi: Oxford University Press.

Central Bureau of Statistics. (1911). *Population census*. Kathmandu: National Planning Commission.

Central Bureau of Statistics. (1952/1954). *Population census*. Kathmandu: National Planning Commission.

Central Bureau of Statistics. (1961). *Population census*. Kathmandu: National Planning Commission.

Central Bureau of Statistics. (1971). *Population census*. Kathmandu: National Planning Commission.

Central Bureau of Statistics. (1981). *Population census*. Kathmandu: National Planning Commission.

Central Bureau of Statistics. (1991). *Population census*. Kathmandu: National Planning Commission.

Central Bureau of Statistics. (2001). *Population census*. Kathmandu: National Planning Commission.

Central Bureau of Statistics. (2001). *Population of Nepal*. Kathmandu: National Planning Commission.

Central Bureau of Statistics. (2003). *Population monograph of Nepal volume 1*. Kathmandu: National Planning Commission and UNFPA.

Central Bureau of Statistics. (2010). *Ganak nirdesika ('Enumerators Guidelines')*. Kathmandu: National Planning Commission.

Central Bureau of Statistics. (2011). *Population of Nepal*. Kathmandu: National Planning Commission.

Central Bureau of Statistics. (2012). *National population and housing census-2011*. Kathmandu: Central Bureau of Statistics, National Planning Commission (NPC).

Central Bureau of Statistics. (2014). *Population monograph of Nepal volume 2*. Kathmandu: National Planning Commission and UNFPA.

Clyne, M., & Ball, M. (1990). English as a lingua franca, especially in industry. *Australian Review of Applied Linguistics*, Series S, No. 7, 1–15.

Cochran, J. L., McCallum, R. S., & Bell, S. M. (2010). Three A's: How do attributions, attitudes, and aptitude contribute to foreign language learning? *Foreign Language Annals, 43*(4), 566–582.

Creswell, J. W. (2012). *Research design: Qualitative, quantitative, and mixed methods approach* (4th ed.). SAGE Publications.

Crystal, D. (2000). *Language death.* Cambridge: Cambridge University Press.

Denzin, N. K., & Lincoln, Y. S. (2011). *The SAGE handbook of qualitative research* (4th ed.). SAGE Publications.

Devkota, K. R. (2018). Navigating exclusionary-inclusion: Experience of Dalit school children in rural Nepal. *Globe: Journal of Language, Culture and Communication, 6,* 106–120. Alborg: Alborg University Press.

Dhakal, D. N. (2014). Contact induced change in Baram. *North East Indian linguistics, 6,* 167–190. Canberra: Australian National University.

Duranti, A. (2001). *Linguistic anthropology: A reader.* Wiley Blackwell.

Dyers, C. (1997). An investigation into current attitudes toward English at the University of the Western Cape. *Per Linguam, 13*(1), 29–38.

Dyers, C., & Abongdia, J. F. (2010). An exploration of the relationship between language attitudes and ideologies in a study of Francophone students of English in Cameroon. *Journal of Multilingual and Multicultural Development, 31*(2), 119–134.

Eagle, S. (2000). The language situation in Nepal. In R. B. Baldauf & R. B. Kaplan (Eds.), *Language Planning in Nepal, Taiwan and Sweden* (pp. 170–225). Sydney: Multilingual Matters Ltd.

Eberhard, G., Gary, S., & Charles, F. (Eds.). (2020). *Ethnologue: Languages of the world* (23rd ed.). Dallas, Texas: SIL.

Edwards, J. (1985). *Language, society and identity.* Oxford, UK: Blackwell.

Edwards, J. (1994). *Multilingualism.* London, UK: Routledge.

Edwards, J. (1999). Refining our understanding of language attitudes. *Journal of Language and Social Psychology, 18*(1), 101–110.

Edwards, J. (2010). *Minority languages and group identity: Cases and categories.* Amsterdam: John Benjamins Publishing Company.

Edwards, V. (2004). *Multilingualism in the English speaking world: Pedigree of nations.* Oxford: Wiley-Blackwell.

Eppele, J., Paul, L., Regmi, D. R., & Yadava, Y. P. (Eds.). (2012). *Ethnologue: Languages of Nepal.* Kathmandu: Central Department of Linguistics and SIL International.

Errington, J. (2000). Indonesian ('s) authority. In P. V. Kroskrity (Ed.), *Regimes of language* (pp. 205–227). Santa Fe, NM: School of American Research Press.

Fabrigar, L. R., MacDonald, T. K., & Wegener, D. T. (2005). The structure of attitudes. In D. Albarracín, B. T. Johnson, & M. P. Zanna (Eds.), *The handbook of attitude* (pp. 79–124). Mahwah, NJ: Lawrence Erlbaum Associates.

Far, M., & Song, J. (2011). Language ideologies and policies: Multilingualism and Education. *Language and linguistics Compass, 5*(9), 650–665.

Fasold, R. (1984). *The sociolinguistics of society.* Oxford, UK: Blackwell.

Fazio, R. H., Chen, J., Mc Donel, E. C., & Sherman, S. J. (1982). Attitude accessibility, attitude-behavior consistency and the strength of the object-evaluation association. *Journal of Experimental Social Psychology, 18,* 339–357.

Fazio, R. H., & Olson, M. A. (2003). Implicit measures in social cognition research: Their meaning and use. *Annual Review of Psychology, 54*(1), 297–327.

Fishbein, M., & Ajzen, I. (1975). *Belief attitude, intention and behavior: An introduction to theory and research.* London, UK: Addison-Wels.

Fishman, J. A. (1972). *The sociology of language: An interdisciplinary social science approach to language in society.* Rowley, MA: Newbury House.

Fishman, J. A. (1991). *Reversing language shift: Theoretical and empirical foundations of assistance to threatened languages.* Clevedon, UK: Multilingual Matters.

Flick. (2009). *An introduction to qualitative research* (4th ed.). Thousand Oaks, CA: Sage Publications Ltd..

Gal, S. (1989). Language and political economy. *Annual Review of Anthropology, 18,* 345–367.

Gal, S. (1998). Multiplicity and contestation among linguistic ideologies. In K. Woolard & B. Schieffelin (Eds.), *Language ideologies: Practice and theory* (pp. 317–331). Oxford: Oxford University Press.

Gal, S. (2002). A semiotics of the public/private distinction. *Differences: A Journal of Feminist Cultural Studies, 13*(1), 77–95.

Gal, S. (2006). Contradictions of standard language in Europe: Implications for the study of practices and publics. *Social Anthropology, 14*(2), 163–181. European Association of Social Anthropologist UK.

Gal, S., & Woolard, K. (1995). Constructing languages and publics: Authority and representations. *Pragmatics, 5*(2), 129–138.

Gal, S., & Woolard, K. (2001). *Languages and publics. The making of authority.* Manchester: St. Jerome's.

Gardner, R. C. (1985). *Social psychology and second language learning: The role of attitudes and motivation.* London, UK: Edward Arnold.

Gardner, R. C. (1991). Attitudes and motivation in second language learning. In A. G. Reynolds (Ed.), *Bilingualism, multiculturalism and second language learning* (pp. 43–62). Hillsdale, NJ: Lawrence Erlbaum Associates.

Gardner-Chloros, P. (2007). Multilingualism of autochthonous minorities. In P. Auer & L. Wei (Eds.), *Handbook of multilingualism and multilingual communication* (pp. 469–492). Berlin, Germany: Walter de Gruyter.

Garrett, P. (2001). Language attitudes and sociolinguistics. *Journal of Sociolinguistics, 5*(4), 626–631.

Garrett, P. (2004). Language contact and contact languages. In A. Duranti (Ed.), *A companion to linguistic anthropology.* Blackwell Publishing Ltd..

Garrett, P. (2005). What a language is good for: Language socialization, language shift, and the persistence of code-specific genres in St. Lucia. *Language in Society, 34*(3). Cambridge, Cambridge University Press.

Garrett, P. (2010). *Attitudes to language.* Cambridge: Cambridge University Press.

Gautam, B. L. (2012). Contact Nepali in Kathmandu valley: Convergence between TB & IA languages. *Nepalese Linguistics, 27,* 38–42.

Gautam, B. L. (2017). Language use and attitude among the Sherpa speaking community in Kathmandu valley. *Gipan, 3*(2), 26–37. Kathmandu, Central Department of linguistics, TU.

Gautam, B. L. (2018a). Language shift in Newar: A case study in the Kathmandu valley. *Nepalese Linguistics, 33*(1), 33–42.

Gautam, B. L. (2018b). Language shift in Sherpa. *Interdisciplinary Journal of Linguistics (IJL), 11,* 119–129. University of Kashmir, India.

Gautam, B. L. (2019). Sociolinguistic survey of Nepalese languages: A critical evaluation. *Language Ecology, 3*(2), 190–208. John Benjamin's Publishing Company.

Gautam, B. L. (2020). *Language contact in Kathmandu.* An unpublished PhD dissertation, Tribhuvan University, Kathmandu.

Gautam, B. L., & Sapkota, S. (2005). A linguistic analysis of online communication. In *Contemporary Issues in Nepalese linguistics Vol. 21,* a journal of the Linguistic Society of Nepal (LSN).

Gawronski, B. (2007). Attitudes can be measured! But what is an attitude? *Social Cognition, 25*(5), 573–581.

Genetti, C. (1999). Variation in the agreement in the Nepali finite verb. In Y. Yadava & W. W. Glover (Eds.), *Topics in Nepalese linguistics* (pp. 542–556). Kathmandu: Royal Nepal Academy.

Gibbons, J., & Ramirez, E. (2004). Different beliefs: Beliefs and the maintenance of a minority language. *Journal of Language and Social Psychology, 23*(1), 99–117.

Giles, H., & Billings, A. (2004). Assessing language attitudes: Speaker evaluation studies. In A. Davies & C. Elder (Eds.), *The handbook of applied linguistics* (pp. 187–205). Oxford, UK: Blackwell Publishing.

Government of Nepal. (2015). *The constitution of Nepal 2015.* Kathmandu: Minister of Law and Justice.

Grenoble, L. A. (2006). *Saving languages: An Introduction to language revitalization.* Cambridge: Cambridge University Press.

Grenoble, L. A., & Whaley, L. J. (1998). Toward a typology of language endangerment. In L. A. Grenoble & L. J. Whaley (Eds.), *Endangered languages: Language loss and community response.* New York: Cambridge University Press.

Grinevald, C. (1998). Language contact and language degeneration. In F. Coulmas (Ed.), *The handbook of sociolinguistics* (pp. 257–270). Oxford: Blackwell Publishing.

Gumperz, J. J. (1982). *Language and social identity.* Cambridge, UK: Cambridge University Press.

Gurung, G. (1985). *Nepalko rajnitima adekhai sachai (Hidden truth in Nepalese politics).* Kathmandu: Gopal Gurung.

Gurung, H. (2002). *Janagananaa-2001 anusaar jaatiya tathyaank: prarambhik lekhaajokhaa* (Primary statistics of ethnicity according to census 2001). Kathmandu: Dhramodaya Sabha.

Hachhethu, K. (2003). Democracy and nationalism: Interface between state and Ethnicity in Nepal. *Contribution to Nepalese Studies, 30,* 217–252.

Haris, R. (2006). *New ethnicities and language use.* New York: Palgrave Macmillan.

Harvey, D. (2005). *A brief history of neoliberalism.* Oxford: OUP.

Heath, S. B. (1989). Language ideology. In *International encyclopedia of communications.* New York: Oxford University Press.

Heller, M. (2000). Bilingualism identity in the post-modern world. *Estudios de sociolingüística, 1*(2), 9–24.

Heller, M. (2003a). Globalization, the new economy, and the commodification of language and identity. *Journal of Sociolinguistics, 7*(4), 473–492.

Heller, M. (2003b). The commodification of language. *The Annual Review of Anthropology, 39,* 101–114.

Hildebrandt, A. K. (2008). *How low can you go? Contact in manange* (Sino-Tibetan, Nepal). Retrieved from http/www.google.com.

HMG. (1990). *The constitution of Nepal 1990.* Kathmandu: His Majesty's Government, Ministry of Law and Justice.

Hock, H. H., & Basir, E. (Eds.). (2016). *The language and linguistics of south Asia.* New York: Mouton de Gruyter.

Hogg, M. A., Abrams, D., Otten, S., & Hinkle, S. (2004). The social identity perspective: Inter group relations, self-conception, and small groups. *Small Group Research, 35,* 246–276.

Hugoniot, K. (1997). *A sociolinguistic profile of the dialects of Maithili.* Kathmandu: SIL.

Hunter, W. W. (1978). *A comparative dictionary of the languages of India and high Asia.* New Delhi: Cosmo Publications.

Hutt, M. (2004). Introduction: Monarchy, democracy, and Maoism in Nepal. In M. Hutt (Ed.), *Himalayan people's war: Nepal's Maoist rebellion.* UK: C. Hurst & Co. Ltd..

Ianos, M. A. (2014). *Language attitude in a multilingual and multicultural context: The case of autochthonous and immigrant students in Catalonia.* Unpublished doctoral dissertation, University of Lleida, France.

Internet World State. (2011). Internet world states news Number 069. Retrieved from www.internetworldstats.com.

Irvine, J. T. (1989). When talk isn't cheap: Language and political economy. *American Ethnologist, 16*(2), 248–267.

Irvine, J. T., & Gal, S. (2000). Language ideology and linguistic differentiation. In P. V. Kroskrity (Ed.), *Regimes of language: Ideologies, polities, and identities* (pp. 35–84). Santa Fe, NM: School of American Research Press.

Irvine, J. T., & Gal, S. (2009). Language-ideological processes. In N. Coupland & A. Jaworski (Eds.), *The new sociolinguistics reader*. UK: Palgrave Macmillan.

Jaffe, A. (2009). *Stance: Sociolinguistic perspectives*. Oxford: Oxford University Press.

Jha, S. (1958). *The formation of the Maithili language*. London: Luzac & Co..

Jha, U. (1989). *Maithili vayakaran aa aur rachana*. Bharati Bhawan Publishers and Distributors.

Johnson, S., & Tomaso, M. M. (Eds.). (2010). *Language ideologies and media discourse: Text, practice & policies*. Continuum International Publishing Group.

Johnstone, B. (2000). *Qualitative methods in sociolinguistics*. Oxford: Oxford University Press.

Jorgensen, D. L. (1989). *Participant observation: A methodology for human studies*. Newbury Park, CA: Sage.

Jupp, T. C., Robert, C., & Gumperz, J. C. (1982). Language and disadvantage: The hidden process. In J. J. Gumperz (Ed.), *Language and social identity*. Cambridge, UK: Cambridge University Press.

Kansakar, T. R. (1996). Multilingualism and the language situation in Nepal. *Linguistics of the Tibeto-Berman Area, 19*(2), 17–30.

Kansakar, T. R. (2011). *A sociolinguistic survey of Newar language*. A report submitted to Linguistic Survey of Nepal, Central Department of Linguistics, Kathmandu.

Kerswill, P. (2006). Migration and language. In K. Mattheier, U. Ammon, & P. Trudgil (Eds.), *Sociolinguistics: An international handbook of the science of language and society* (Vol. 3, 2nd ed., pp. 1–27). Berlin: Walter De Gruyter.

Khubchandani, L. M. (1978). Multilingual education in India. In B. Spolsky & R. L. Cooper (Eds.), *Case studies in bilingual education*. Rowley, MA: Newbury House.

Kroskrity, P. V. (2000). Regimenting languages: Language ideological perspectives. In P. V. Kroskrity (Ed.), *Regimes of language: Ideologies, polities, and identities*. Santa Fe, NM: School of American Research Press.

Kroskrity, P. V. (2004). Language ideologies. In A. Duranti (Ed.), *A companion to linguistic anthropology* (pp. 496–517). Oxford: Blackwell.

Kroskrity, P. V. (2009). Language renewal as sites of language ideological struggle: The need for ideological clarification. In J. Reyhner & L. Lockard (Eds.), *Indigenous language revitalization: Encouragement, guidance and lessons learned* (pp. 71–83). Flagstaff, Arizona: Northern Arizona University.

Kroskrity, P. V. (2010). *Language ideologies: Handbook of pragmatics*. London: John Benjamin Publishing Company.

Labov, W. (1972). *Sociolinguistic pattern*. Philadelphia: University of Pennsylvania Press.

Lambert, W. E. (1974). Culture and language as factors in learning and education. In F. F. Aboud & R. D. Meade (Eds.), *Cultural factors in learning and education*. Bellingham, WA: Western Washington State University.

Lambert, W. E., Hodgson, R. C., Gardner, R. C., & Fillenbaum, S. (1960). Evolutional reactions to spoken languages. *Journal of Abnormal and Social Psychology, 60*(1), 44–51.

Lasagabaster, D. (2003). Attitudes towards English in the Basque autonomous community. *World Englishes, 22*(4), 585–597.

Lasagabaster, D. (2005). Attitudes towards Basque, Spanish and English: An analysis of the most influential variables. *Journal of Multilingual and Multicultural Development, 26*(4), 296–316.

Li, W. (2006). *The bilingualism reader*. New York: Routledge.

Lincoln, Y. S., & Guba, E. G. (1985). *Naturalistic inquiry*. Newbury Park, CA: Sage.

Lippi-Green, R. (1997). *English with an accent: Language, ideology, and discrimination in the United States*. London and New York: Routledge.

Maddox, B. (2003). Language policy, modernist ambivalence and social exclusion: A case study of Rupandehi district in Nepal's terai. *Studies in Nepali History and Society, 8*(2), 205–224.

Makihara, M. (2007). Linguistic purism in Rapa Nui political discourse. In M. Makihara & B. B. Shiefflin (Eds.), *Consequences of contact: Language ideologies and socio-cultural transformations in Pacific societies*. London: Oxford University Press.

Makihara, M., & Schieffelin, B. (2007). *Consequences of contact: Language ideologies and socio-cultural transformations in Pacific societies*. London: Oxford University Press.

Malla, K. P. (2015). *From Literature to culture: Selected writings on Nepalese studies, 1980–2010*. Kathmandu: Social Science Baha.

Masica, C. P. (1976). *Defining a linguistic area*. Chicago and London: University of Chicago Press.

Masica, C. P. (1991). *The Indo-Aryan languages*. Cambridge: Cambridge University Press.

May, S. (2012). *Language and minority rights: Ethnicity, nationalism and the politics of language* (2nd ed.). New York, NY: Routledge.

Milroy, J., & Milroy, L. (1985). Linguistic change, social network and speaker innovation. *Journal of Linguistics, 21*, 339–384.

Myers-Scotton, C. (2006). *Multiple voices: An introduction of bilingualism*. Oxford and Malden, MA: Blackwell.

Nakayiza, J. (2013). *The sociolinguistics of multilingualism in Uganda: A case study of the official and non-official language policy, planning and management of Luruuri-Lunyara and Luganda*. PhD thesis, SOAS University of London.

Nepali, G. S. (1965). *The Newars: An ethno-sociological study of a Himalayan community*. Bombay: United Asia Publications.

NEPC. (1956). *Education in Nepal*. Report of the Nepal Education Planning Commission, Nepal.

Nettle, D., & Romaine, S. (2000). *Vanishing voices: The extinction of the world's languages*. Oxford: Oxford University Press.

Neupane, D. P. (2010). Nepalko bhasa niti: Bigat bartaman ra aagami sandarva (Nepali language policy: Past, present and future perspectives). *Udvodh, 1*(1), 82–87. Dharan, Sunsari: Nepal University Progressive Teachers' Association, Mahendra Multiple Campus Unit.

Noonan. (2008). *Genetic classification and language contact*. Retrieved from http/www.google.com.

Noonan, M. (2003). Recent language contact in the Nepal Himalaya. In D. Bradley, R. Lapolla, B. Michailovsky, & G. Thurgood (Eds.), *Language variation: Papers on variation and change in the Sinosphere and in the Indosphere in Honour of James A Matisoff* (pp. 65–88). Canberra: Pacific Linguistics.

Olson, J. M., & Maio, G. R. (2003). Attitudes in social behavior. In T. Millon & M. J. Lerner (Eds.), *Handbook of psychology, personality and social psychology* (pp. 299–326). New Jersey, NJ: John Wiley & Sons.

Olson, J. M., & Stone, J. (2005). The influence of behavior on attitudes. In D. Albarracín, B. T. Johnson, & M. P. Zanna (Eds.), *The handbook of attitude* (pp. 223–272). Mahwah, NJ: Lawrence Erlbaum Associates.

Paudel, K. P. (2009). *Ethnicity and language issue in the present context in Nepal*. A paper presented at CET Seminar at Sukuna Multiple Campus, Indrapur, Morang.

Phyak, P. (2016). *For our Cho:tlung: Decolonizing language ideologies and (Re) imaging multilingual education policies and practices in Nepal*. Unpublished PhD dissertation, University of Hawai at Manoa.

Piller, I. (2011). *Intercultural communication: A critical introduction*. Edinburgh: Edinburgh University Press.

Piller, I. (2015). Language ideologies. In *The International encyclopedia of language and social interaction*. https://doi.org/10.1002/9781118611463/wbielsi140.

Piller, I. (2016). *Linguistic diversity and social justice: An introduction to applied sociolinguistics*. Oxford: Oxford University Press.

Piller, I., & Cho, J. (2013). Neoliberalism as language policy. *Language in Society, 42*(1), 23–44.

Pradhan, J. (2006). Language shift in Newar. In *Nepalese linguistics*, Vol. 22. Kathmandu: Linguistic Society of Nepal.

Pradhan, K. (1991). *The Gorkha Conquest: The processes and consequences of the unification of Nepal, with particular reference to eastern Nepal*. Calcutta: Oxford University Press.

Pradhan, U. (2018). Simultaneous identities: Ethnicity and nationalism in mother tongue education in Nepal. In *Nations and Nationalism* (pp. 1–21). ASEN/ John Wiley& Sons Ltd.

Rana, B. K. (2008). Recent change and development in different language communities in Nepal. In J. W. Mohammad (Ed.), *Linguistic dynamism in South Asia*. New Delhi: Gyan Publishing House.

Regmi, D. R. (2013). Contact induced change in Bhujel. *Nepalese Linguistics, 28*, 167–177. Kathmandu, Linguistic Society of Nepal.

Regmi, D. R. (2017). Convalescing the endangered languages in Nepal: Policy, practice and challenges. *Gipan, 3*(1), 139–149. Kathmandu, Central Department of Linguistics.

Riaz, A., & Basu, S. (2007). *Paradise lost? State failure in Nepal*. UK: Lexington Books.

Ricento, T. (Ed.). (2000). *Ideology, politics and language policies: Focus on English*. Amsterdam and Philadelphia: John Benjamin Publishing Company.

Ricento, T. (Ed.). (2015). *Language policy and political economy: English in a global context*. Oxford and New York: Oxford University Press.

Sallabank, J. (2013). *Attitudes to endangered languages: Identities and Policies*. New York: Cambridge University Press.

Sayer, P. (2015). Expanding global language education in public primary schools: The national English programme in Mexico. *Language, culture and curriculum, 28*(3), 257–275.

Scotton, C.-M. (2002). *Linguistics: Bilingual contact encounters and grammatical outcomes*. Oxford: Oxford University Press.

Scotton, C.-M. (2005). *Multiple voices: An introduction to bilingualism*. Wiley-Blackwell.

Seel, A., Yadava, Y. P., & Kadel, S. (2015). *Medium of instruction and languages of Education (MILE): Ways forward for education policy, planning, and practice in Nepal: Final report*. A report submitted to the Ministry of Education, Nepal and DFID.

Shah, R. K. (2012). *Code switching in Maithili language (A case study in Siraha district)*. An unpublished MA thesis, Tribhuvan University, Nepal.

Sharma, B., & Phyak, P. (2017). Neoliberalism, linguistic commodification, and ethno linguistic identity in multilingual Nepal. In *Language in Society* 1–26. Cambridge University Press.

Sharma, G. (2000). *Nepalko saikshik itihash (Academic history of Nepal)*. Kathmandu: Lumbini Pustak Bhandar.

Silverstein, M. (1979). Language structure and linguistic ideology. In P. R. Clyne, W. F. Hanks, & C. L. Hofbauer (Eds.), *The elements: A para session on linguistic units and levels* (pp. 193–247). Chicago: Chicago Linguistic Society.

Sonntag, K. S. (1995). Ethnolinguistic identity and language policy in Nepal. *Nationalism and Ethnic Politics, 1*(4), 116–128.

Sonntag, K. S. (2007). Change and permanence in language politics in Nepal. In A. B. M. Tsui & J. Tollefson (Eds.), *Language policy, culture, and identity in Asian contexts* (pp. 205–217). Mahwah: Lawrence Erlbaum.

Spolsky, B. (2009). *Language management*. New York: Cambridge University Press.

Tajfel, H., & Turner, J. C. (1979). An integrative theory of intergroup conflict. In W. G. Austin & S. Worchel (Eds.), *The social psychology of intergroup relations* (pp. 33–47). Monterey, CA: Brooks/Cole.

Taylor, S., & Bogdan, R. (1998). *Introduction to qualitative research methods: A guide book and resource* (3rd ed.). Hoboken, NJ: John Wiley & Sons Incl.

Thapa, R., Luitel, B., Gautam, B. L., & Devkota, K. R. (2018). *Language shift in Nepal: A general study*. A report submitted to Language Commission Nepal, Kathmandu.

Thomason, S. G. (2001). *Language contact: An introduction*. Edinburgh: Edinburgh University Press.

Thomsen, C. J., Lavine, H., & Kounios, J. (1996). Social value and attitude concepts in semantic memory: Relational structure, concept strength, and the fan effect. *Social Cognition, 14*, 191–225.

Tollefson, J. W. (2013). *Language policies in education: Critical issues* (2nd ed.). New York: Routledge.

Tucker, R. (1998). A global perspective on multilingualism and multilingual education. In J. Cenoz & F. Genesee (Eds.), *Beyond bilingualism. Multilingualism and multilingual education* (pp. 3–15). Clevedon, UK: Multilingual Matters.

Tumbahang, G. B. (2009). Process of democratization and linguistic human rights in Nepal. *Tribhuvan University Journal, XXVI*, 8–16.

Turin, M. (2005). Language endangerment and linguistic rights in the Himalayas: A case study from Nepal. *Mountain Research and Development, 25*(1), 4–9. International Mountain Society.

Turin, M. (2007). *Linguistic diversity and the preservation of endangered languages: A case study from Nepal*. Kathmandu: ICIMOD.

Turner, J. C. (1982). Towards a cognitive redefinition of the social group. In H. Tajfel (Ed.), *Social identity and intergroup relations* (pp. 15–40). Cambridge, UK: Cambridge University Press.

Turner, R. L. (Ed.). (1985a). Indo Aryan linguistics: Collected papers (1912–1972). In *The Infinitive in Nepali* (pp. 76–87). Delhi: Disha Publications.

Turner, R. L. (Ed.). (1985b). Indo Aryan linguistics: Collected papers (1912–1972). In *Further Specimen in Nepali* (pp. 156–172). Delhi: Disha Publications.

UNESCO. (2003). *Language vitality and endangerment*. Document submitted to the International expert meeting on UNESCO program safeguarding of endangered languages. Paris: USESCO.

Warriner, D. S. (2015). "Here, without English, you are dead" Ideologies of languages and discourses of neoliberalism in adult English language learning. *Journal of Multilingual and Multicultural Development, 37*(5), 495–508. Taylor and Francis.

Weinrich, U. (1953). *Languages in contact: Findings and problems.* Hague, the Netherlands: Mouton.

Wolcott, H. F. (2002). Writing up qualitative research better. *Qualitative Health Research, 2*(1), 91–103.

Wolfram, W., & Schilling-Estes, N. (2006). *American English: Dialects and variation* (2nd ed.). Malden, MA: Blackwell.

Wood, W. (2000). Attitude change: Persuasion and social influence. *Annual Review of Psychology, 51*, 539–570. https://doi.org/10.1146/annurev.psych.51.1.539.

Woolard, K., & Schieffelin, B. B. (1994). Language ideology. *Annual Review of Anthropology, 23*, 55–82.

Woolard, K. A. (2003). We don't speaks Catalan because we are marginalized: Ethnic and class meanings of language in Barcelona. In R. K. Blot (Ed.), *Language and social identity* (pp. 85–103). Westport, CT: Praeger.

Woolard, K. A. (2009). Linguistic consciousness among adolescents in Catalonia: A case study from the Barcelona urban area in longitudinal perspective. *Perspective, 22*, 125–149.

Yadav. (2015). *Code mixing in Maithili Nepali.* An unpublished MA thesis, Tribhuvan University, Nepal.

Yadav, R. (2013). *Language shift in Maithili speakers: A case study in Kathmandu valley.* An unpublished MA thesis, Tribhuvan University, Nepal.

Yadava, Y. P. (2007). Linguistic diversity in Nepal perspectives on language policy. A paper presented in a seminar *Constitutionalism and diversity in Nepal* organized by CNAS, TU 22–24 August: Kathmandu, Nepal.

Yadava, Y. P. (2014). Language use in Nepal. In *Population monograph* (Vol. II, pp. 51–72). Kathmandu: CBS and UNFPA.

Yadava, Y. P., & Glover, W. (Eds.). (1998). *Topics in Nepalese linguistics.* Kathmandu: Royal Nepal Academy.

Yadava, Y. P., & Turin, M. (2005). Indigenous languages of Nepal: A critical analysis of linguistic situation and contemporary issues. In Y. Prasad Yadava & P. Lal Bajracharya (Eds.), *Indigenous languages of Nepal: Situation, policy planning and coordination.* Kathmandu: NFDIN.

INDEX

© The Author(s), under exclusive license to Springer Nature
Switzerland AG 2021
B. L. Gautam, *Language Contact in Nepal*,
https://doi.org/10.1007/978-3-030-68810-3